Make It Mine!

By Alexa Keating

Copyright 2011 Alexa Keating

Prologue

'Make It Mine' is not just a book about home decorating; but it does provide a wonderful, lighthearted approach to decorating your home!

It creates an awareness of how our state of mind affects the world we live in, confirming the old adage that while "You may never reach the summit, and for that you will be forgiven; but if you don't make at least one serious attempt to get above the snow line you will always regret it!"

'Make It Mine' delves into the psyche so subtly that one barely notices they have been given a 'checkup from the neck up' about why we live the way we do in our own homes!

The book is filled with funny stories, sad stories and a million tips, tricks and ideas to help you navigate from a house to a home!

It is full of ideas and solutions for everyone from the college student to retirees. **The ideas are bold, not old stuff.**

For motivating, inspiring ideas that teach you how to prevent becoming a victim as you locate and improve your home in today's economy; this is a must read! This book is funny and happy, and is a worthwhile, down to earth endeavor that will bear wonderful fruit.

It is filled with profound thoughts, inspiration and practical ideas for successful living.

Table of Contents

Dedication

This book was inspired by and written for all the people who have a house or apartment and wish it could be their dream home. There's a difference.

You have inspired me and many others to reach higher, and grow farther in the search to help create new ideas and better methods; once unheard of.

To every **'Make it Mine'** warrior who jumps in, and dares to dream and to act, I applaud your efforts. I'm proud of you! You will be too!

For the many people who taught me lessons, and who encouraged and nudged me to write this book; I know what part you have played in this coming to fruition. I appreciate your efforts and your encouragement.

You all know who you are!

Chapter 1
A' Huntin' We Will Go!

The 'perfect' place; whether you're a first time home hunter, apartment seeker or a veteran buyer, the search is on! Some things never change!

It's a process that begins with a clear idea of what is perfect, meets a new companion named reality and changes constantly until you've finally arrived at the "This is it!" decision.

Before you execute any paperwork, review Chapter 2, 'Signed, Sealed, Delivered, I'm Yours'.

It is so much easier to avoid potholes than to dig out and repair the damage from them!

Having spent thirty plus years in the real estate, new construction, remodeling and residential and commercial decorating industries, I have enjoyed the opportunity to participate in almost every process of the 'perfect' home search with literally thousands of people, from every walk of life.

Things I learned with and from them
are worth a check and review:

Quick Check Steps

a) Take an honest look at your income
and budget; if you are able to stay within
the 25% range for your mortgage or rent
payment you will find the other areas of
your life far more manageable and
enjoyable.

b) If you plan to rent or lease a
property get familiar with the general
terms that are acceptable in your area
including typical deposits required, credit
and income requirements and terms of
leases available. Every area is different.

c) If you plan to purchase a property,
a pre-approval of financing is helpful in
determining what amount and terms a
lender will approve you for.

This helps you set the limit for
purchase price in addition to being a big
boost in getting your offer accepted once
you have made your final selection.

d) Relax, take a deep breath and keep
your sense of humor. Build good
memories to share from your search!

e) Location, location, location; never
detour from this cardinal rule; regardless

of whether you are renting or purchasing. Spend some time deciding where you feel comfortable; and which area *in your comfort range* is affordable and offers the things you believe are not negotiable. (This is tricky - we'll take a longer look at that later.)

f) Safety; if you are a single female your safety concerns are different than two or three guys sharing an apartment. Keep your safety concerns at the top of your list. Children require a whole different set of safety issues, ditto for pets. This should always be on your non-negotiable list.

g) Hunt with your head - not your heart; in the next few chapters you will see many ways to change spaces and make them perfect for you and your lifestyle!

h) Obstacles, obstacles, obstacles; when this begins to be the 'norm' in your dream, let go. If this is the right home for you it will happen fairly smoothly. I have to share this true story as the example that I learned early in my real estate career, and never forgot.

It Seemed Impossible   After three years as a Realtor, I opened my own office; listings are a must for any realtor, even more critical when the business is new and your inventory is zero.

While I had enjoyed incredible success in sales, one particular home had been listed with my previous broker for a year and a half with worse than dismal results; we couldn't give it away.

There simply was no reason the home did not sell. Every agent in the office had open houses at the home and it was shown repeatedly by other companies.

The home was a seven room brick ranch with fireplace, family room, two car garage, three bedrooms, and two baths.

All this on a three quarter acre fenced lot with an assumable loan (no credit check required back then) and a payment of $356.00 including taxes and insurance! It required only $6000.00 down to purchase on those terms.

Remarkably, it was priced $10,000 under market, was in perfect condition and in a highly desirable area and very close to schools. How could this home not sell? In utter frustration, the owners stopped trying and took it off the market.

I stopped there first to get a listing for my new company. The owners were disheartened and told me they had only listed the home originally because they had fallen in love with an older two story home in the historic district; one which had long since been sold.

I needed listings and sales! I asked them for a 24 hour listing conditioned on my being able to secure the home they originally wanted to purchase; a long shot but I literally had nothing to lose!

They said yes, obviously believing it was not possible to accomplish this mission.

I went to the historic home and asked if they were interested in selling their home. I explained the situation with the buyer who had wanted to purchase their home and lost it to them when they were not able to sell their home.

The owner had two very large dogs and advised me that they had taken the historic home because they also had lost the one they had wanted to purchase!

The home they wanted had two and a half acres and was perfect for their children and dogs but was taken off the market suddenly.

They would only sell this home if they were able to buy the one they originally wanted. They signed a conditional listing agreement and a purchase agreement for the home they lost. This was fast becoming a quest!

Off I went to the home with the acreage. The woman who answered the door was really surprised to hear my story.

She explained that she and her husband had lived in the house for many years and went together to find a new construction home with less yard maintenance due to their increasing age.

They found one they loved and put their house on the market, only to learn almost immediately that her husband had a terminal illness.

They took it off the market and dedicated their time to his declining health. By the time I arrived at the home, her husband had died.

She desperately wanted to leave the memory of his dying there; and to let go of the acreage that required so much time for a single, aging woman.

And, you guessed it; she wanted the new home they had chosen together.

This same process was repeated. She signed a conditional listing agreement and we went together to look at the new subdivision.

We were able to find the exact home on a different lot which she found acceptable.

Things may seem to be looking great at this point; all the listings were sold and everyone was headed to the home they had always wanted.

Except, all of this was conditioned on selling the first home that had been on the market for a year and half!

Selling the first home, with a really sad track record, was now the basis of all these people's dreams coming true.

I went home that evening, knowing I had 24 hours to sell a home that had the worst possible chance of a 24 hour sale. It was a pretty tough order.

But then, I was not in charge.

Later that evening I received a call from a former school mate. She was looking for their first home, and they required a few things that she felt would make it difficult.

Her wish list; three bedrooms, a family room, a two car garage for her husband who was a mechanic, a large yard for her three sons and, although she believed it was impossible; a fireplace and a fenced yard were on her wish list.

There's more; they had credit issues and needed a loan assumption, could only afford $375.00 a month with taxes and insurance included and only had $5600.00 to put down.

Their desired school district was the very one the house I needed to sell was located in.

Maybe you can see where this is going. We met at the house; both of their parents came along. No one believed this was possible.

They saw this home that no one would buy as the answer to their prayers. The parents helped complete the down payment and in one single day all of these people realized a dream!

What changed? Timing; that's all.

The moral of this story is that when things get really hard, it is either not the right home or not the right time.

Universal law unfailingly delivers on the promise that 'You cannot lose what is yours; you cannot keep what is not.' You may find this to be true in every area of your life! I have.

If it's too tough, examine why that might be.

Step back and be willing to let go if necessary. It will return in a workable way with terms that will suit your needs if it is yours.

Just know that the right home is there for you, and when you find it, things get easy!

What Counts?

Unless you are blessed with an unlimited budget and funds are not an issue, learn to take a good look at the bones of the homes or apartments in your search.

If the layout works with your lifestyle, and the room sizes fit you or your family's requirements, anything is possible.

We'll talk about how to make that work in apartments and rental homes too!

Another Lesson

I had the opportunity to work with my brother, who was a building contractor, for many years. It was during the boom in south Florida in 2004 that I learned why people clamored to buy his homes.

He had always been enormously successful, and his homes were in great demand. I was charged with the sales and marketing strategy for his homes; so his method that was so loved by the public was particularly interesting to me.

My brother insisted on meeting with every buyer personally. This was a little unusual, as most builders simply review the purchase agreement and accept or reject the terms. On occasion they meet the buyer at the time of purchase. I was surprised to learn what was most important to him in those meetings.

While the typical builder may review his plans with buyers and answer questions, my brother took a different approach; carefully questioning each buyer about their lifestyle.

He asked each buyer to tell him about their life, to walk through a typical day in their family's life and how they lived.0

From that information he helped guide them to the design that best suited their family's lifestyle. This process began with asking them to start a typical morning at home, it continued through the day, even to mentally pulling into the driveway and getting out of the car after work, to bedtime; including laundry, TV time to bedtime.

With this information he was able to determine traffic flow, the value of a 'mud room' off the garage, the number of baths the home needed to accommodate the family and the layout of the space that would allow the family to gain the greatest quality time in the home.

He learned all of this from mentally walking through a typical day in their lives and how their time was spent.

Nothing was impossible to him, not moving a wall or enlarging or decreasing a room size or the entire home.

The important issue was that THEY could live comfortably there; he knew this would result in them loving their home, and that it would work for everyone involved.

Give this process some thought in your search.

It worked beautifully for him and for every buyer. Before you commit, take the time to visually live in the home before making a decision.

The "bones" are the most important aspect in how comfortable you or your family will be once you have chosen the location.

If you have a small budget and changes don't seem likely, keep reading!

Chapter 17 'Barely Get Along Street' explores a variety of possibilities that may seem unattainable; this opens many opportunities for you have what you need to create a perfect space. Really!

Fear not! It's all about the bones; everything else can be changed.

h) Finally; take a good look at your current furnishings. If you purchased them or selected your home furnished, the 'look and feel' appeals to you and speaks volumes about what you like and feel comfortable with.

We're going to spend a lot more time on furnishings, but you will probably discover that what you have chosen in the past is what you are going to be drawn to in the future.

It is a reflection of your personal taste; our challenge is to make it work with your dream.

Pay attention to the check list and your search will be easier to narrow and define. Include someone who supports your dream and the hunt will be fruitful.

Home should be a 'feel good' place that you can't wait to get back to and enjoy.

Many things play into creating this, but it all starts with locating **THE PLACE!**

Chapter 2
Signed, Sealed, Delivered...
I'm Yours!

It's that time now, the search is over; you've found the one! Great!

Let's visit a new friend named reality!

It is sad but true that new issues need to be examined as sometimes hidden obstacles crop up in home hunting. The following tips may be more important than the search results in the hunt.

Please take the time to review the list and complete your own due diligence before proceeding. I promise life will be much sweeter if you do.

Buyers Beware!

a) Even if you are using a realtor, before signing your purchase agreement, run, don't walk to your computer, click onto your favorite search engine and find your local County Property Appraisers office. There you will find all the details on the home you are looking at.

This begins with a property data search and will include current and previous owner's names, addresses, previous purchase prices, all permits that have been issued on the property (great for learning what has been a problem and what has been replaced) and all of the property tax history.

This search also provides the appraisal details at the time the home was built, including square footage and almost everything that matters from then to the present. Bear in mind that property values on the site are based on tax values which are less than the market value.

b) Once you have that information, take a look online at your local county Clerk of Courts office. There you can enter the owners names and complete a public records search. Why? You will learn whether the home is in a foreclosure action and anything that has been filed against the property.

This is important when writing your offer. You need all of the facts to protect yourself.

Real Estate 101 says *'Caveat Emptor' or let the buyer beware.* **So, be aware!**

c) If you don't own a computer or know how to use one, find a friend who does. It's worth the search.

d) When there is no possible way to do your own online search; call. The records are public; and a simple call to the County Property Appraiser's office and to the Clerk of Courts will provide the answer to all of the pertinent questions.

Renters Roadblocks

a) Thought you were out of the danger zone because you are a tenant? Think again! The rules are slightly different for signing a lease agreement in a community (apartment or condo) versus an agreement on a single family home or duplex.

b) The checklist for an <u>apartment community</u> begins with your search.

While you are at the property look carefully at the grounds. Are they well maintained? Is the grass cut, parking lot in a good state of repair, gates functioning properly? Do things seem shipshape? Then continue your search there.

Typically when you are visiting an apartment community you will be shown their 'model.' This is a great way to see how furnishings will fit, and a lousy way to see how they maintain the units.

The models are never exposed to day to day living and therefore are always maintained in 'new' condition. Insist on seeing the actual unit you will be leasing before executing a lease.

Apartment dwellers normally enjoy an added protection; because of the number of people who may be affected if the owners of the community are in default, the courts appoint a trustee who will ensure that the tenants are protected, repairs are made and vital things like water and sewer are paid. That's a plus.

You can follow the same advice provided under Buyers Beware to see if the community is in default before making a final selection.

The Gate Caper

If you think this isn't important, I have to share my own experience to show you why it may be:

As my spunky little mom began her eighties we searched for a safe and secure apartment community that would permit her to keep her beloved little dog.

I made a temporary detour to stay with her soon after. On the surface, this community appeared to be a perfect place that offered the security of gates, peaceful wooded areas and the infamous Florida lakes throughout the community.

One evening as I approached the gate in my little BMW Z4 (the gates were frequently torn off by people who apparently did not have the access card or grew weary of waiting for them to work) I passed through the gates, felt a lurch and then watched in horror as the front bumper of my car was nearly ripped off.

The gate was torn off; the automatic arm (black and not visible at night) was still attached and swinging back and forth at will.

It swung out and latched itself onto the low front bumper that is characteristic on the Z4 car and presto, my bumper became attached to the arm and firmly under control of the whim of the swinging arm!

I dragged the partially attached bumper with me to the nearest parking area; a sister took me to the auto parts store to buy anchors to hold the bumper to the under girdle of the car so it could be moved to our assigned space.

The next morning I indignantly approached the office with my complaint.

They unceremoniously marched me to the front of the gate where a 'Not Responsible' notice was posted. This sign was invisible at night; and, it applied equally to tenants.

It really did not matter to them whether or not this was legal; this little paradise was well on the way to insolvency, unbeknown to us.

Had we paid attention to the air conditioning that frequently froze up and stopped working, (a critical situation in the summer in south Florida) and the plumbing that seemed to always require a 'patch,' we would not have been so surprised at the outcome.

On my final exit from the community I limped through yet another broken gate; my little 'James Bond' car rapidly beginning to resemble your typical junk mobile.

Maintenance matters!

c) A condo community is maintained by the condo association. In some ways it is less protected than the apartment communities.

When an association is not able to collect on the association fees due to pending or actual foreclosure actions; their ability to maintain grounds and roads is severely hampered. Their problems become your problems.

Follow the same advice provided in the apartment community and then one more:

d) Condos are individually owned, just like a single family home. The association is responsible for the maintenance of the exterior of the properties, grounds and roads; however, each unit is sold and purchased in the same exact manner as a typical house.

Make sure to visit the Buyers Beware section of Chapter 1, every part of it!

Condos place you in the same foreclosure risk position as houses; a surprise like that can result in your 'dream home' becoming an unexpected 48 hour notice to move; delivered by the sheriff. That is a painful and avoidable experience. If you find evidence of any foreclosure action, move on, not in!

If you have just discovered that your landlord is in foreclosure, head right back to your computer and your favorite search engine.

Type in your county, state and the words tenants + foreclosure on the search bar; carefully read the laws and see how they apply to your situation.

The less information you provide, both in the search engine box and especially at the County Property Appraiser's site, the more information you will find.

Stay with the bare minimum information like the *number of the home and the street only* (no Street, Avenue or Court at the end of the address) and then select the proper link that applies to your home and your situation.

The Sunshine State

Florida was in the throes of the mass foreclosure actions. The number of people who were victimized by this was unusually high.

The state legislature passed laws that offered an umbrella of protection to the tenants, forcing the person or bank who acquired the home at the public sale to offer several months to the tenant to continue renting while they arranged a move; or a settlement amount to assist in their move.

Your state may not have these laws but whatever they are, they apply to you.

If you've just received the notice, look for the same information and proceed accordingly.

If you cannot locate the information you need, check with your County Prosecutor's office.

They know the law and how it applies to your situation and will usually, very briefly, tell you what you need to know.

If it's a true 48 hour notice, find boxes, friends who will help, and look for a storage facility that offers specials like Public Storage where the first month is only one dollar.

Large movers are scheduled much further out than 48 hours, so plan on a DIY (do it yourself) move with friends, rental trucks or a smaller local mover who may be available.

If you find yourself in this situation, don't waste too much time ranting about how much you will sue the owner for.

If he or she is in a foreclosure action, they already have someone bigger than you in line to collect; the bank!

For now, shake it off and make haste; there's a lot to do and a little time to do it in.

You've just joined the ranks of a brand new kind of 'public education.' If a change is coming, let's look at how to make it happen; as painlessly as possible.

Special Needs Solutions

Yankee Ingenuity is a wonderful part of our American Heritage! I strongly encourage every nation to adopt this 'can do' policy beginning in their elementary school classes.

What's it all about? As my sons loved to remind me, 'No does not mean no!' There is almost always a way to convert a no to a yes when you're on the home hunt.

I don't qualify – If you visited your bank and received a pre-approval letter to purchase a home, you can skip this one.

a) <u>Apartments </u> – There's a new game in town that is probably a result of the mass of foreclosures and the damage it has caused to many people's credit ratings.

Most apartment communities now offer the option of high risk insurance that is purchased after they determine that your credit does not meet their minimum requirements.

It is surprisingly affordable. If they do not tell you about this option, ask. It works like the credit card companies that collect an annual fee to cover the risk.

b) Many apartment communities accept an additional month of security deposit to cover the increased risk. This is a great solution if you are not cash strapped and utterly worthless if you are.

c) They may offer a co-signor opportunity. Proceed with great caution if you choose this method. Friends become enemies if things do not work out well. I suggest you move on to a privately owned property with no realtor involvement when you arrive at this option.

<u>Renting directly from the owner</u> – Have a care here. These people are taking a risk and using their good judgment to trust you with their property. They have become a disappearing breed.

Honor them; they are fast becoming extinct, with many choosing to hand the risk over to a realtor, thereby increasing the cost of the rent.

a) Rent rates and terms can be negotiated with a private owner much easier that a management company.

b) If you are handy or willing to care for the lawn or pool, or to make improvements to the property, the rates can easily be reduced by the costs they are incurring to provide these for you.

c) Credit is not normally a big issue if you can verify your income to meet the rental rate; and provide credible references.

d) If you genuinely feel like this is the home you want to own, ask about a lease purchase option.

This allows you to re-build credit on an agreement to purchase, credits a portion of the rent each month to your down payment, and does not require a pre-approval on credit or income.

The owner benefits by handing over maintenance of the property to you, the purchaser.

e) Investor financing – In most states, investors have been on a buying spree; grabbing the ridiculously cheap foreclosure homes and adding them to their increasing portfolio.

The down payment is normally higher for this purchase, however, the investor acts as the lender, collects an amortized payment and you own the home with very little qualifying requirements.

Having examined all of your options you should now be ready to make a good decision, sign the papers and call this one home.

The fun begins now.

Chapter 3
Movin and a Groovin!

We'll keep this short and sweet. Moving is a necessity after making your selection. No one likes it; but it has to be done.

There are some handy ideas that you may not know, so this could be worth a review.

a) If your move is long distance you have fewer choices.

Some people simply elect to sell everything and start over in the new location. If you love your furnishings, there are better ways.

A long distance mover is very expensive. If money is not an issue you may find this the best one for you. It helps if you are in a position where your company has transferred you, and is willing to pay for the move. Lucky you!

A word of caution; I learned the hard way that these movers have very limited coverage for damages. Even if the damages come to thousands of dollars, they may cover only $500.00. The rest is your problem.

b) Most people do not have this option so let's move on to 'other options.' After several moves, I learned that Penske is one of the few companies that currently offer one way moving very affordably.

They do not charge for mileage and offer every size of truck. I like them a lot! If one truck cannot handle your move and you have a willing family member or friend to drive the second truck, you're in luck! Do it!

c) A local move is simpler. I learned that if I could take all the closet items, kitchen items and bathroom boxes in my car and put them away before the move; things got really easy!

The truck comes, the big items are loaded, off loaded and put into place in your new home; and you are moved in. That is slick!

d) Smaller moving companies are in every city. Their prices are very competitive and you can supervise the move.

Look for them in the phone book, the newspaper and on Craig's List. If you are careful, you will discover that Craig's List is full of good people, on an honest mission. I have had many really good experiences with movers from Craig's List.

e) Last, and certainly more common is the 'gather your friends' method. You simply invite them over to help pack and move, buy a dinner when it's over and pray they still call you a friend! Usually, they do, and you will be called on to return the favor.

Happy hauling! Once again, relax, smile and remember; this too will pass!

Whether you have just unloaded the truck or merely decided to claim your space and make it distinctly yours, welcome to the best part of being home!

Moving Checklist

Two Months Before

Sort and purge Go through every room of your house and decide what you'd like to keep and what you can get rid of. Think about whether any items will require special packing or extra insurance coverage.

Research Start investigating the moving companies you are considering, their options and benefits. Do not rely on a quote over the phone; request an on-site estimate. Get an estimate in writing from each company, and make sure it has a USDOT (U.S. Department of Transportation) number on it.

Create a moving binder. Use this binder to keep track of everything—all your estimates, your receipts, and an inventory of all the items you're moving.

Organize school records. Go to your children's school and arrange for their records to be transferred to their new school district.

Six Weeks Before

Order supplies; including boxes, tape, bubble wrap, and permanent markers. Don't forget to order specialty containers, such as dish barrel boxes or wardrobe boxes.

Use it or lose it Start using up things that you don't want to move, like frozen or perishable foods and cleaning supplies.

Take measurements Check room dimensions at your new home, if possible, and make sure larger pieces of furniture will fit through the door.

One Month Before

Choose your mover and confirm the arrangements. Select a company and get written confirmation of your moving date, costs, and other details.

Begin packing Start packing the things that you use most infrequently, such as the waffle iron and croquet set. While packing, note items of special value that might require additional insurance from your moving company. Make sure to declare, in writing, any items valued over $100 per pound, such as a computer.

Label Clearly label and number each box with its contents and the room it's destined for. This will help you to keep an inventory of your belongings. Pack and label "essentials," boxes of items you'll need right away.

Separate valuables Add items such as jewelry and important files to a safe box that you'll personally transport to your new home. Make sure to put the mover's estimate in this box. You'll need it for reference on moving day.

Complete a change of address Go to your local post office and fill out a change-of-address form, or do it online at usps.gov. But in case there are stragglers, it's always wise to ask a close neighbor to look out for mail after you've moved. Check in with him or her two weeks after the move, and again two weeks after that.

Notify important parties Alert the following of your move: banks, brokerage firms, your employer's human resources department, magazine and newspapers you subscribe to, and credit card, insurance, and utility companies.

Forward medical records Arrange for medical records to be sent to any new health-care providers or obtain copies of them yourself. Ask for referrals.

Two Weeks Before

Arrange to be off from work on moving day. Notify your office that you plan to supervise the move and therefore need the day off.

Tune up Take your car to a garage, and ask the mechanic to consider what services might be needed if you're moving to a new climate.

Clean out your safe-deposit box If you'll be changing banks, remove the contents of your safe-deposit box and put them in the safe box that you'll take with you on moving day.

Contact the moving company Reconfirm the arrangements.

One Week Before

Refill prescriptions Stock up on prescriptions you'll need during the next couple of weeks.

Pack your suitcases Aim to finish your general packing a few days before your moving date. Then pack suitcases for everyone in the family with enough clothes to wear for a few days.

A Few Days Before
Defrost the freezer If your refrigerator is moving with you, make sure to empty, clean, and defrost it at least 24 hours before moving day.

Double-check the details Reconfirm the moving company's arrival time and other specifics and make sure you have prepared exact, written directions to your new home for the staff. Include contact information, such as your cell phone number.

Plan for the payment If you haven't already arranged to pay your mover with a credit card, get a money order, cashier's check, or cash for payment and tip. If the staff has done a good job, 10 to 15 percent of the total fee is a good tip. If your move was especially difficult, you might tip each mover up to $100. Don't forget that refreshments are always appreciated.

Moving Day

Verify Make sure that the moving truck that shows up is from the company you hired: The USDOT number painted on its side should match the number on the estimate you were given. Scams are not unheard-of.

Take inventory Before the movers leave, sign the bill of lading/inventory list and keep a copy.

Now, take a deep breath and congratulate yourself on completing this big change.

Chapter 4
Color Your World!

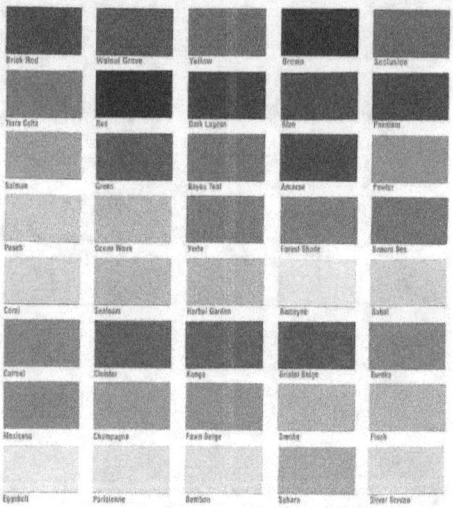

Cozy, comfortable, elegant,
masculine, sunny, bright, beautiful... every
room is a statement! Much like the artist
beginning a new painting, treat your walls
like a canvas and begin to paint a picture
with color first. Paint is the least
expensive method to create the greatest
change.

Where does it start?

There's a method to the madness that everyone needs to understand to successfully create the feeling you want to project.

If you simply cannot imagine what color makes you feel good, walk around in stores, model homes and your friend's homes; pay attention to each room and how it 'feels' when you walk into the space.

Colors have feelings!

Walk into the rooms in your home and imagine how you want them to 'feel.' Then consider the following as you make the final selection. To sum it up:

Red

Physiological Effect: Red has been shown to increase blood pressure and stimulate the adrenal glands. The stimulation of the adrenals glands helps us become strong and increases our stamina. Pink, a lighter shade of red, helps muscles relax.

Psychological Effect: While red has proven to be a color of vitality and ambition it has been shown to be associated with anger. Sometimes red can be useful in dispelling negative thoughts, but it can also make one irritable. Pink has the opposite effect of red.

Pink induces feelings of calm, protection, warmth and nurturing. This color can be used to lessen irritation and aggression as it is connected with feelings of love. Red is sometimes associated with sexuality, whereas pink is associated with unselfish love.

Red is a highly energetic color. Take a look around fast food restaurants like McDonald's and you will frequently see reds and deep yellows. The subliminal message is 'hurry up and hurry out.' The more people they move, happily, through the restaurant the more they can serve.

If you are considering using red tones in your home keep in mind that it should be contained to a high energy area unless you have a careful plan to seduce your partner. We'll discuss that later in this book; the effects of colors, not seducing your partner!

Pink evokes a completely different feeling even though it is a shade of red. Little girls love it in every shade from Fuchsia to pale ice pink. It is a feel good, warm color. I try to avoid pinks or gender colors in master bedrooms.

Orange

Physiological Effect: Orange has proven to be a stimulus of the sexual organs. Also, it can be beneficial to the digestive system and can strengthen the immune system.

Psychological Effect: Orange has shown to have only positive effects on your emotional state. This color relieves feelings of self-pity, lack of self-worth and unwillingness to forgive. Orange opens your emotions and is a terrific antidepressant.

Orange is another high energy color. This color is sensual and sets a mood of sharing and playtime. The tangerine shades are warm and can be inviting in many areas. The deeper shades now available like the 'Olympic Grecian Leather' can actually set a sophisticated mood with white or light furniture.

Yellow

Physiological Effect: Yellow has proven to stimulate the brain. This stimulation can make you more alert and decisive. This color makes muscles more energetic and activates the lymph system.

Psychological Effect: Similarly to Orange, Yellow is a happy and uplifting color. It can also be associated with intellectual thinking: discernment, memory, clear thinking, decision-making and good judgment. Also affects aiding organization, understanding of different points of view.

Yellow builds self-confidence and encourages optimism. However, a dull yellow can bring on feelings of fear.

Yellow tends to work best in kitchens where a sunny wakeup call is inviting, in bathrooms to create a light hearted feeling and in children's playrooms.

This color energizes; you may want to reconsider a pure yellow in children's bedrooms for that very reason.

Gold Tones are popular shades that run from the palest gold tones to the deep gingerroot tones typically used to create a Mediterranean feel.

The soft tones are warm and relaxing, the deeper ones are more calming but all work well with darker furniture tones, metals and brown accessories.

In small rooms prepare to be overwhelmed by dark gold tones. The exception to this rule is using it in half baths where accessories can create an entirely different feeling.

Green

Physiological Effect: Green is said to be good for your heart. On a physical and emotional level, green helps your heart bring you physical equilibrium and relaxation. Green relaxes our muscles and helps us breathe deeper and slower.

Psychological Effect: Green creates feelings of comfort, laziness, relaxation and calmness. It helps us balance and soothe our emotions. Some attribute this to its connection with nature and our natural feelings of affiliation with the natural world when experiencing the color green.

Yet, **darker and grayer greens can have the opposite effect**. These olive green colors remind us of decay and death and can actually have a detrimental effect on physical and emotional health. Note that sickened cartoon characters always turn green.

Green is the comeback kid in colors. It has been widely used in those awful hospital rooms, avocado appliances we would rather forget and now in lime that makes an interesting, if faddish, statement.

Gray greens are very calming, allowing the accessories to make the statement and set the 'mood.'

Teals, or blue greens, lead us to a tropical paradise feeling if combined with accessories that complete that look. Think gentle ocean breezes or even tropical evening skies when considering this color.

Be careful when choosing the shade of teal for offices or places where you want to accomplish work tasks. You will probably not want to do it.

Blue

Physiological Effect: In contrast to red, blue proves to lower blood pressure. Blue can be linked to the throat and thyroid gland. Blue also has a very cooling and soothing affect, often making us calmer. Deep blue stimulates the pituitary gland, which then regulates our sleep patterns. This deeper blue also has proved to help the skeletal structure in keeping bone marrow healthy.

Psychological Effect: We usually associate the color blue with the night and thus we feel relaxed and calmed. Lighter blues make us feel quite and away from the rush of the day. These colors can be useful in eliminating insomnia. Like yellow, blue inspires mental control, clarity and creativity. However, too much dark blue can be depressing.

Blue is a love it or hate it color. In its palest shades it evokes calm and cool emotions.

Dark Blue, when combined with the right accessories, can be beautiful if the room is large enough to use this color for the 'canvas.' In master suites with all white accessories it becomes a paradise to relax in. Blue is the favorite color selection in all ethnic groups.

Purple

Physiological Effect: Violet has shown to alleviate conditions such as sunburn due to its purifying and antiseptic effect. This color also suppresses hunger and balances the body's metabolism. Indigo, a lighter purple, has been used by doctors in Texas as an anesthesia in minor operations because of its narcotic "A soothing or numbing agent affiliation."

Psychological Effect: Purples have been used in the care of mental or nervous disorders because they have shown to help balance the mind and transform obsessions and fears. Indigo is often associated with the right side of the brain; stimulating intuition and imagination.

Violet is associated with bringing peace and combating shock and fear. Violet has a cleansing effect with emotional disturbances. Also, this color is related to sensitivity to beauty, high ideals and stimulates creativity, spirituality and compassion. Psychic power and protection has also been associated with violet.

Purple is a warm color that evokes a feeling of royalty, velvet, and beautiful sunsets. It is a balancing color that heals and yet stimulates creativity.

Brown

Psychological Effect: Brown is the color of the earth and ultimately home. This color brings feelings of stability and security. Sometimes brown can also be associated with withholding emotion and retreating from the world.

Psychological Effect: Brown is a bold color that makes a bold statement. It has a stabilizing effect; however, the way it is used will determine the actual affect. In large rooms with light wood or white trim it can create a warm and energizing feeling.

Beige, Taupe and light neutral shades of brown are a warmer shade of white. These colors make a perfect neutral backdrop and can feel warm or impersonal depending on the way you use furnishings and accessories.

If you are in doubt you will find that these colors or a very light brown/gray shade will match almost any furniture and set a neutral tone.

White

Psychological Effect: White is the color of ultimate purity. This color brings feelings of peace and comfort while it dispels shock and despair.

White can be used to give you a feeling of freedom and uncluttered openness. Too much white can give feelings of separation and can be cold and instill the feeling of isolation.

Show me a home or apartment with plain white walls, pictures hung high by the ceiling and furniture lined against the walls and I would like to introduce you to the **'House of Commons!'**

White is cooling, calming and sometimes sophisticated; it can also feel cold, devoid of emotion and boring.

The same room transforms to sophisticated, soothing and beautiful when you add textured white window coverings, sumptuous white and contrasting rugs and throw pillows and a bold sofa. If this is combined with black and white photos you will feel like you have walked onto a movie set.

Be careful with a decision to paint everything white. Later we will talk about accessories and textures and how they affect your paint choice.

Gray

Psychological Effect: Gray is the color of independence and self-reliance, although usually thought of as a negative color. It can be the color of evasion and non-commitment (since it is neither black nor white.) Gray indicates separation, lack of involvement and ultimately loneliness; unless...

Shades of Gray; Lighter shades of gray, with white tones, work perfectly with furniture that does not have browns as a primary color. This creates a soft and cool tone in the room.

Dark gray becomes a sophisticated backdrop when mixed with white or dark wood trim in the room.

Black is a bold, dramatic, confident and sophisticated color. It is a primary color and yet the attributes of both white and gray are felt in various shades of black. It is sometimes cold. Use it sparingly unless you have a serious plan for the entire room.

Everything is crystal clear now, right? It helps to envision the room bathed in your color selection. Close your eyes and 'feel' the room, visually place your favorite furniture or accessories in the space; then select the color that delivers the message you want to project.

Painting is a task that most people can perform at some level. If you are fortunate enough to be able to afford a painter you will likely make that choice.

Many painting contractors are looking for work since the housing and new construction market has become so depressed.

This means pricing is negotiable. Don't pass on this idea until you try pricing the job unless your budget does not accommodate the possibility.

If you intend to paint the rooms yourself (I always have) there are a few tips that will make your project run smoothly and produce results you can be proud of.

a) **Choose a good, dependable paint**. Satin or eggshell paint creates a soft and nearly flat appearance that does not show defects in the wall.

This happens because it has no sheen; light does not reflect off of it. Keep that in mind when choosing the color, you may want to slightly lighten the shade.

The washable flat paint also hides imperfections and works nicely with the Shabby Chic look. It is a little more expensive so weigh the benefits against the cost and then decide what works best for your budget.

b) **Cover the floors**, even if you think they are easy to clean or not really important. You'll be glad you did when clean up time is upon you.

c) If you are not completely comfortable with your trim brush, **tape, tape and tape again**.

d) **Buy good paint rollers** and the right length of roller covers. You really do get what you pay for in the paint materials.

e) **Great brushes** (horsehair if possible, with thin tapered edges) are the easiest to get a perfect edge on the trim work.

I was given the opportunity to learn from a professional and discovered that taking a long look at the angle of the wall and where it meets the ceiling is vital to know which way to set the brush on the wall and trim it out.

Stand back and take a good look at the angles of the walls and the ceiling and set the brush down with the bare tip of the brush at the point where the wall meets the ceiling.

f) **Roll the walls in (W) patterns** and back again. This is one time when straight lines will not be your friend. The more directions you roll in, the smoother the overall finish will be.

g) **Use enamel paint on trim work**. It wears beautifully and washes easily. It is also a pain to work with as it is almost never washable and turpentine will become a new friend.

h) **I try to avoid semi gloss finishes.** They are dated, show every imperfection on the walls and attract attention to the walls rather than letting them be the canvas they should be.

Who knew there was so much emotion in a simple can of paint? Make your selection and be brave; the results are so worth the effort.

If you are renting, get permission to paint and be prepared to repaint the walls to white when you leave.

I refuse to rent a property I cannot paint; I know it is essential to feeling like I live in a home, not a house. Besides, however can we create a masterpiece if we have no canvas?

Chapter 5
When Chaos is King!

Look around; if this does not apply to your own home I bet you know someone this glove fits!

Chaos in a home is evident when there is no specific place for shoes, clothing, books, TV remotes and a host of other things.

I can't tell you how many times I have walked into a home like this and listened to the host who relates one of the following causes:

a) **"No one listens**; the kids refuse to help and I can't do this by myself."

b) **"My partner won't help!** He or she is a slob and has no respect for the things that are important to me."

c) **"I'm busy**! I don't have time to be a slave to a house."

d) **"I'm no maid;** why should I pick up after everyone? No one does it for me!"

e) **"I don't care.** Houses are just not that important to me!"

f) **"I had to clean house all of my life!** My mother made me clean hers and my kids can do ours!" (More common that you know) Imagine hearing, "This house is a mess! The kids haven't cleaned yet!" And, it feels right to the person who is saying this to you.

g) **"I spent a lot of years getting my education and degree; I have way**

too much on the ball to worry about housework". (This is a VIP syndrome)

h) **"I hate housework! Who cares?"**

There are lot's more; these are the ones I most frequently hear. **Catch a clue here**; these people have some things in common!

1) **There is an underlying anger** issue in nearly every statement. Someone feels used or abused!

2) **People are confused** about time issues; what takes their time and what wastes their time.

3) **Declining health** issues have begun and normal maintenance, upkeep and housekeeping have become too difficult to perform.

4) **Most people who have chaos in their home are overwhelmed.** They can't 'see the reaching' and the task seems daunting. What's the use of digging in if it won't make a difference?

5) **There is usually chaos in some other important area of the lives of people who choose to live like this.** Your surroundings reflect your state of consciousness.

Your home is the biggest investment you will likely make and the one place charged with providing comfort to you and your family.

That's why it is referred to as your castle in general; and why the US Constitution takes so much care to protect your rights with respect to your home.

It's important! Let's find the method to make you fall in love with it again!

Chapter 3 is a short chapter that is devoted to the 'On the Move' issue. If you are in that position it is the best place to start.

If you move into a home and create order, you will enjoy far more harmony in the space and not have to tear down the chaos that has accumulated.

Most people are not on the move; they're already there. Spend a short time examining why chaos reigns supreme in your home.

One by one, let's examine the most typical 'reasons' people provide; then we can visit getting a new perspective on this issue!

Solutions to Consider

a)"No one listens; the kids refuse to help and I can't do this by myself."

Chaos, in and of itself, creates the 'no one listens' attitude. Everyone feels overwhelmed, no one knows where to start and no one can see the finish line.

Therefore, everyone refuses to waste their time helping achieve something they believe is not possible. This becomes a habit! After some time passes it becomes, "This is how we live."

Someone has to 'step up' and begin the change process. It is a little tougher when you are feeling overwhelmed but things happen quickly once you commit to it.

One at a time – this is the process. I like to start at the front door; you choose your most important starting point.

Many people who exhibit the 'It's no one's business how my house looks' attitude scoff at the front door process. I can't understand why these people don't see that they and their family use the same door! Who doesn't want to be warmly welcomed at their front door?

If you can't imagine where to start I like to empty the room. Leave the furniture if you don't have the space to move it out, but move it to the center of the room. Then clear the room, pictures and all.

It's a new point of beginning. Look at the walls and windows. This is a great time to take stock of wall colors.

Soothing neutral earth tone colors set the tone of warmth and coziness. If you don't have one on your walls try to find $20.00 in your budget and buy paint.

Clean the woodwork and windowsills, and then move to the windows. Sparkling clean windows allows natural light to penetrate the gloom.

Clean the floor. Then tackle the overhead lighting or fans. Chapter 9 'Let There Be Light' is devoted to how to select lighting that fits your personal style and budget and creates the feeling you want to inspire in your room.

It may be worth jumping to Chapter 9 as you tackle this issue.

A lack of storage is the chief offender in chaos. Either you can't find it or never used it! It's time.

First take a long and honest look at the things you have removed from your room. What falls into the 'clutter' pile and what is important to you?

Eliminate the clutter. I find it to be easier to leave it in the pile I have moved out of the room and follow this process until every room is finished. Then make the final decision as to whether it is a 'must keep item' or can leave your life gracefully.

Check out the <u>Furniture Placement chapter</u> in this book and get some ideas as to how it affects the room.

Look at what your want to create and then be bold! Try some different furniture placement ideas and find the one the best suits you.

After the first room is complete, this becomes a natural process to move through the home and eliminate chaos and clutter. So dig in!

b) **"My partner won't help! He or she is a slob and has no respect for the things that are important to me."**

This is one of those underlying anger issues we talked about!

It is work examining why you feel that way and why your partner chooses to ignore your feelings. We don't cover this in the 'Make It Mine' book.

Come to an agreement that is respectful to both of you and make a commitment to honor the agreement.

Then visit the a) No One Listens solutions above and dig in to alter the course of chaos and regain your peace of mind.

c) **"I'm busy! I don't have time to be a slave to a house."**

Imagine that! You have time to spend needless wasted hours hunting for important papers, shoes, lost clothing, keys and a multitude of other important things you need.

This causes countless explanations to others beginning with the 'I can't find it but as soon as I locate it I'll let you know' story to the 'It's gone; I don't know how that is possible but I've looked everywhere to no avail' excuse.

You're too busy? Really, you're too busy?

Visit the 'a) No One Listens' solutions section and recover hours of wasted time. If you're really busy you don't have time to waste on needless searches. You become a slave to your unwillingness to participate in your success.

Getting order back into your home will bring order to your life. Things just get simple and you'll have a lot more time to spend on the things you want to squeeze into your schedule.

d) "I'm no maid; why should I pick up after everyone? No one does it for me!"

This is another underlying anger issue!

No one wants to feel like a maid in their own home. No one wants to be the only one who cares about things being in place either.

There is a sense of unfairness playing out here.

If this is how you really feel it is time for a family council meeting. Every member of the household should attend; let everyone 'vent' their own feelings.

Every person in the home is entitled to some measure of respect for their feelings, even the children. If you instill the attitude that respect is important at a young age your children will never forget it as they grow into adulthood. It is a valuable characteristic.

Then begin to form an agreement about how the family would like their space to feel and how to arrive at that point.

No matter what the reasons are, unless you are addressing a specific room and the occupant's unwillingness to perform duties, everyone will probably begin at the point of 'a) No One Listens.'

Visit that section and follow the ideas there when you are ready to begin.

e) "I don't care. Houses are just not that important to me!"

I wonder why? You are willing to spend a large part of your income to supply a roof over your head and yet, it's just not that important.

Examine why you feel that way. Everyone dreams of having their own space, a private place to call 'mine.' If you feel your home is not important, you may want to reconsider this one. Many times it really means, 'I am overwhelmed and do not know where to start!' Studies in human nature have proven that not knowing what to do will usually result in doing nothing.

Take heart; revisit the 'a) No One Listens' solutions above and start reclaiming control of your space. You'll be glad you did!

f) "I had to clean house all of my life! My mother made me clean hers and my kids can clean mine!" (This is more common that you know) Imagine hearing, "This house is a mess! The kids haven't cleaned it yet!" And, it feels right to the person who is saying this to you.

This one is particularly disturbing to me. Imagine how many times a day we say, "You're just a child, you can't make those kinds of decisions."

And yet, the most important investment of our lives is turned over to the same children who are too young to decide what to have on their dinner plate.

If your parents placed you in this position, remember how overwhelmed it made you feel.

Many times families encounter abrupt changes; divorce, a death of a parent or illness of one of the parents, and things change quickly. It may seem natural to just 'let the kids' do the tasks.

For a temporary solution this may be fine; tell them it is temporary and why it is. And then, look for help from family or friends for the things you cannot do.

I hope you will reconsider this position and step up and reclaim the adult part of this responsibility.

If not, you may create generations of abused children who grow up resentful and angry about their homes instead of appreciating the opportunity to claim personal space and enjoy it.

I urge you to visit the 'a) No One listens' solutions and bring the family together by providing a well loved place to call home.

g) **"I spent a lot of years getting my education and degree; I have way too much on the ball to worry about housework."** (This is a VIP syndrome)

You may be surprised at how many people parrot this attitude.

If keeping this attitude is important to you, then I sincerely hope you have managed to turn all that education into enough income to pay someone else to maintain control of your home.

That is, if you are willing to turn the reins over to someone else. I'm not. Rarely do people have 'too much on the ball' to live in harmony in their home.

Examine this attitude closely; maybe you just need to think about what is really important to you and then prioritize your home at or near the top of the list.

You also need to visit 'a) No One Listens' solutions and either dig in yourself or supervise someone else in the process.

You have way too much on the ball to live in chaos and disorder that wastes your time!

She was very important!

I once showed up for an open house at a home where the woman felt this way.

Dirty socks and clothing were strewn throughout the home, dishes were piled up so high it was impossible to see the counter space, there was an unpleasant order throughout the home – one that smelled of grime; bathrooms were revolting and bedrooms were piled high with clutter, only the bed was open and available, although unmade.

While it certainly was not my job to clean house I was embarrassed to even allow lookers in the door. A call to my Sales Manager made it clear that I had to stay because the Open House ad was in the paper. For obvious reasons, the home had been on the market for a very long time with no interest. The owner apparently had no interest either!

I spent several minutes picking up the clutter from the floors, ran the dishwater and piled the dirty dishes into the sink, vacuumed the floors, mopped the tiled areas and proceeded to clean bathrooms and wash dishes.

I decided I had pretty much taken over the home at that point so I strategically positioned the furniture.

I was scheduled for a three hour open house; five lookers came through while I was in the process of cleaning it up, and one buyer who saw the finished project. I worked hard for that commission!

The owner should have done the same things months ago and they would have been happily ensconced in their new home much sooner!

There is a little bit of arrogance in this attitude that I have a problem with when I encounter it.

I also have a good education, and I'm sharp enough to know that this kind of clutter and dirt doesn't 'feel' good!

h) **"I hate housework! Who cares?"**
I've learned that once chaos and disorder

are eliminated in a home; all the occupants regain respect for the way it looks and feels.

Why? Because they have regained the lost time searching for things that are never in place because they had no place; and, have honestly enjoyed how their home feels to them and to everyone who comes through the door. It instills a sense of pride. And that's a good thing!

Let's take a moment to look at other causes:

Declining health issues may have begun and normal maintenance, upkeep and housekeeping have become too difficult to perform.

Elderly people do not like to let others know how hard things have become.

It makes them feel even more helpless which is very frightening; they already have begun to see their independence and control in their lives slipping away.

Pay close attention if you notice things are not the same in an elderly persons home. They may be quietly screaming for help and afraid to speak out.

If so, round up the most caring people in their lives and make a plan, with them, to help do the things that you know are important to them on a regular basis.

People who become unexpectedly handicapped feel the same way.

They usually wonder why no one else has noticed what they can't do, but are they are too proud, or in too much pain to speak up.

Chapter 6
Where's Grumble Alley?

"I try to avoid power trips; I find they frequently take me to places I had not intended to go."
~My Mother

Grumble Alley is a lot like that. You just stumble into it and instinctively look for the first exit!

Most people don't ask for directions to 'Grumble Alley.' However, they always remember when they accidently detoured and found themselves there.

In many instances it is located in the same neighborhood as <u>Chaos is King</u>! These two places have a lot in common!

Some people actually live on 'Grumble Alley!'

You've most likely been there too. It happened when you were in a perfectly good mood, your day was going just fine and you were happily looking forward to the rest of your evening when, 'bam' things went south!

On 'Grumble Alley' people are agitated and angry; they shout and find fault with almost everything.

It's like a maze, you get so caught up in the actions of the people and their emotions that you can't find the door; and then your day is ruined too!

Grumble Alley starts when <u>something is off kilter in the space</u>. If you find yourself in 'Grumble Alley' you need to disconnect from the actions of the people, take a deep breath and look around objectively.

The most common causes of this syndrome are:

a) **Paint colors** that are jarring to the sub conscious. At a subliminal level, we react!

b) **Too much furniture improperly placed**, impeding the traffic flow and causing the space to feel disjointed and too full. It is difficult to enjoy a room with these problems; a simple walk through becomes a navigational quest.

c) **No textures in the room**; this makes the space feel unfriendly and cold.

d) **Window treatments that block natural light** and create a 'cave like' feeling in the space.

e) **Lighting that is too harsh** or so low it becomes a challenge to discern the traffic pattern.

Commercial stores are very aware of the effects of this. Great care is taken to properly 'set the tone.'

If you look closely you will see that the cosmetics area has soft pale pinks that instill a feeling of being loved and cared for.

The fragrance area is designed to make you feel confident, rich, bold and sensuous – just like you want their product to make you feel.

The furniture area offers many different kinds of lighting and accessories to create a very different and finished feeling, allowing you to 'visualize' their product in your home.

This practice is carried throughout successfully marketed stores.

When care is not taken to achieve these results you will find you have stumbled into a commercial fright that rapidly becomes 'Grumble Alley.'

The employees are discontented and treat you disrespectfully, customers are equally rude and angry and your day is shot.

People, who seemingly choose to live on 'Grumble Alley,' if they think about how it happened, will discover that they accepted this result as a consequence of allowing chaos to rein in their home and subsequently their lives.

Look around your home; if you see any of these undesirables, kick them to the curb! Say good riddance to bad rubbish and continue your 'Make It Mine' journey!

You'll be glad you did.

Chapter 7

Wide Open Spaces

update. change. rearrange.

In the eighties a 'new' concept of homes became popular. Gone were the square parlors, traditional living rooms, separate dining rooms, isolated kitchens, enclosed family rooms and square bedrooms with small closets! It's all about open spaces now. That's great! Now what?

Open spaces deliver challenges and opportunities simultaneously. Here you are, moved into this new and better home that is open from the front door to the kitchen! What to do?

On the up side, you can choose your dining area. Get creative and see what area feels like a relaxing space; one that has the best view and some access to the delivery of the food will create an easy flow and feel natural.

This floor plan typically defines the builder's idea of the dining area by the placement of the chandelier. That's not a game changer for the 'Make It Mine' warrior.

Lighting is easily changed from room to room if you love the one you're with and with a replacement if you don't.

A note of caution; before you rush out to buy lighting, decide what style, yes style, is your style.

Take a long look at your furniture, your paint selections, your accessories and the look and feel you want to create in each room.

Lighting is one of the most strategic tools in the game plan of creating your masterpiece. Use it wisely to define an entry area, a dining area and any other 'specific' areas in this floor plan.

In this kind of floor plan, living rooms usually need to be created by furniture selections and placement.

Open floor plans are devoid of wall outlets except against the walls which, as you may have noticed, are missing. Attempting to use table lamps will leave you with exposed cords that impede traffic flow and create unnecessary fall risks.

These floor plans work better with floor lighting and wall sconces that promotes a more comfortable and cozy atmosphere.

Storage is another challenge in the open floor plan. Decide whether you want to create an entry area or foyer and work from that point of beginning.

Placing an entry chest or buffet style of furniture at the point where you want to 'end' the entry area will provide a place for paper and pens to jot down notes or messages at the door and a place for sweaters and other light wraps you grab on the way in or out of your home.

Open shelving units will maintain the open feeling, create a break point and still provide some light storage if drawer units are located in the bottom sections. We'll be looking at furnishings and where to find the things that best suit your design ideas later in this book.

This same challenge is encountered in the family room area and can be addressed in the same manner. The best part of an open floor plan is the walls you do not have to relocate!

The open floor plan usually offers "plant shelving" to accommodate floating walls. These become a display area for your most valued treasures that are stored in many attics for lack of a place to show them off safely.

And one more thing; if you have vaulted ceilings you now have very tall walls. Make good use of them! Look for shelving or older free standing cabinetry units; repurpose them and 'hang em high!'

This is a wonderful place to showcase something important in your décor plan.

You can find every style of pre-built fireplaces at your local Lowe's and many other places (back to the online search here) and create your best focal point by placing it under a hanging unit.

You also acquire that much talked about mantle for hanging stockings and a romantic setting for the cozy evenings with this kind of unit. They also have a heater and blower hidden behind the glowing 'fire, making them a very practical solution to a cold room!'

It's a given that having an unlimited budget leaves every door open in your selection. If not, take heart; we have a plan!

We will be devoting a few chapters to furniture placement and how to create specific and defined areas in your home. Those chapters may be very beneficial to you.

Chapter 8
And Tiny Places

show off a streamlined space

Small spaces offer a range of challenges and come in a variety of shapes.

From the graduate exchanging home for a dorm room (and usually sharing it) to studio and efficiency apartment dwellers, cottage or bungalow inhabitants, growing families who are searching for a method to accommodate the changing needs of their family, anyone attempting to find a space for their home office and anyone who lives in cities where space is a premium with a price tag to match; all of you share this challenge.

A castle does not have to have palatial space to feel like a palace.

Dorm Rooms present a special set of issues. You have one room the size of a typical bedroom that must become the 'home space' for two people, include a place to quietly study, relax, enjoy some privacy and provide enough storage for all the 'stuff' young people deem as vital to their happiness. (This includes clothes, shoes, computers, TV's and everything that applies.)

While many dorm rooms come equipped with some basic furniture they rarely work towards creating a home away from home as they imply.

If you are lucky enough to have a good relationship with your room mate, things can get a lot better very affordably.

Shop thrift stores, Craig's List (Under the 'For Sale' section of Craig's List you will find a Free section. This has postings for 'curb alerts' and will allow you to relieve someone of their goods for the price of your gas to pick it up, and that's all) and any other options you can locate. This is a temporary living arrangement; keep your cash for the lean times and get creative!

Put out a BOLO (Be on the lookout for) space saving twin pedestal beds. They take up the same space as the cot you are provided with and offer 6 wide drawers below the bed for expanded storage.

Even if the beds have to be pushed against the wall, you can use the unavailable side for seasonal storage and the important 'stuff' you acquire.

Look for inexpensive open, short shelving units and place them on the closet floor. These will keep spare books, sweaters and jeans easily accessible and leaves the top rod for hanging clothes. Install inexpensive hanging shoe organizers on the interior of the doors.

Look for used night stands that have three drawers. This is not the time or space for the open look. If you do this you will eliminate the need for dressers and open space for one important piece. A desk armoire provides your much needed desk space, built in lighting to study, a place for all of your computer and class book storage and, the all important and must have TV. You can close the door and your room is neat; your area privacy is protected when you've finished your work.

Check out the rules on painting your room. If it is permissible, do it! Take a long look at your windows. Adding soft long drapes adds privacy, texture and creates a cozy feeling. They also keep out unwanted natural light when you plan to sleep in! Find complimentary bedding and throw pillows and thick cushy rugs to complete your theme.

Add neutral lamps to the nightstands or opt for wall sconces by the beds to allow each of you the opportunity to sleep without unwanted lights interfering and your tiny, cramped dorm room will become a true haven away from home.

If you have a roommate who is agreeable you will have fun locating these pieces and redecorating. Even the reluctant roommate may have a different attitude when they see your results!

Studio Apartments consist of one room that accommodates the living and sleeping areas and if you are lucky, a full or partial wall separating the kitchen; and one bath.

Take a moment to review the Dorm Room suggestions to make the most of acquiring storage in your apartment.

You may find a 'Murphy bed' (a fold out bed that appears as a narrow wall unit when closed) is built into the space. If so, it's a great way to get rid of the sleeping area when you're not using it.

If not, you can use the same shopping methods described above to find a used one if you cannot afford a new one.

In lieu of the Murphy bed, a futon is inexpensive, serves as a sofa and folds out to a bed for sleeping. All of these are good space saving options to consider.

Smaller apartment size tables for your living room will allow you to create a spacious feeling in your home. Look for end tables that can double as night stands with three drawers if possible. These will provide storage for clothing and lingerie while serving as end tables during the daytime.

Large, thick wool rugs create a sumptuous and homey feeling in the room and add texture. Look for light, neutral colors to increase the feeling of space.

This also adds a visual break point separating your living area from your dining area.

essential elements

The dining area is probably small but looking for a way to separate it from your living area will make you feel like it's a special area and not an intrusion into the living space.

Look for a small buffet or entry table to place against the end wall. This adds storage for dining linens and anything else you may need. Again, look for drawers! More is better.

Hang a mirror, a special picture or something simple and large above the buffet. Mirrors make the space feel larger.

Once you determine your personal style, look for a 36" table with chairs that slide under the table. This frees up walking space when you are not dining. If you have space for a small tree beside the buffet you will find that it provides a complete separation of the area visually.

Lastly, go to Habitat for Humanity thrift store, consignment stores or any other option where you can locate a gorgeous light to hang above your table. Nothing says an area is special quite so much as the light you grace that space with.

Top your table with a simple and special centerpiece and your eating area is now a dining area that you will love to entertain in.

The kitchen is usually a galley style that has limited floor space. If a microwave is not included in your apartment look for a small one and hang it under a cabinet. Counter space is critical in galley kitchens.

If you have any available space, look for a rolling cart that doubles as a chopping block/prep area and has storage below. You can move it when you're using it and store it out of the way when you're not preparing or cooking food. Use substantial size baskets on the shelf below to store vegetables and fruits.

The keep it simple method will make you feel much less cramped in smaller kitchens. Orderly cabinets increase storage space; clean countertops allow you to use the limited space for food preparation.

Your bath area is likely to be compact. If so, look around. Is there an area to hang a decorative cabinet and increase storage? If so, find one! The biggest challenge in a studio apartment is find a place for the things you require to be comfortable.

If you have a Burlington Coat Factory or Tuesday Morning store near you, they are worth checking out for shower curtains and inexpensive and attractive storage solutions.

A cloth shower curtain will create a warm and cozy feeling even in a small bath area. Thick towels on the towel bars say 'this is my home.' Some things are worth splurging on and I firmly believe these two items are on the top of the list.

Explore the window coverings and paint options described in the <u>Dorm Room</u> section and apply it to your studio apartment if possible.

<u>Efficiency Apartments</u> typically offer a combined living and dining area, a kitchen, separate bedroom and a bath.

Take a moment to review the suggestions in the <u>Dorm Rooms</u> and <u>Studio Apartment</u> sections as they all apply except the sleeping area. You are fortunate to have a completely separate bedroom.

Your bedroom should feel special. You are sharing living and dining spaces; take the time to look for possibilities in your bedroom.

I love to use chandeliers with dimmer switches in bedrooms. You can find really beautiful small chandeliers inexpensively if you shop with the methods we have been discussing in the previous sections.

If that idea does not interest you, look for a really attractive ceiling fan and use the bedside lamps for lighting.

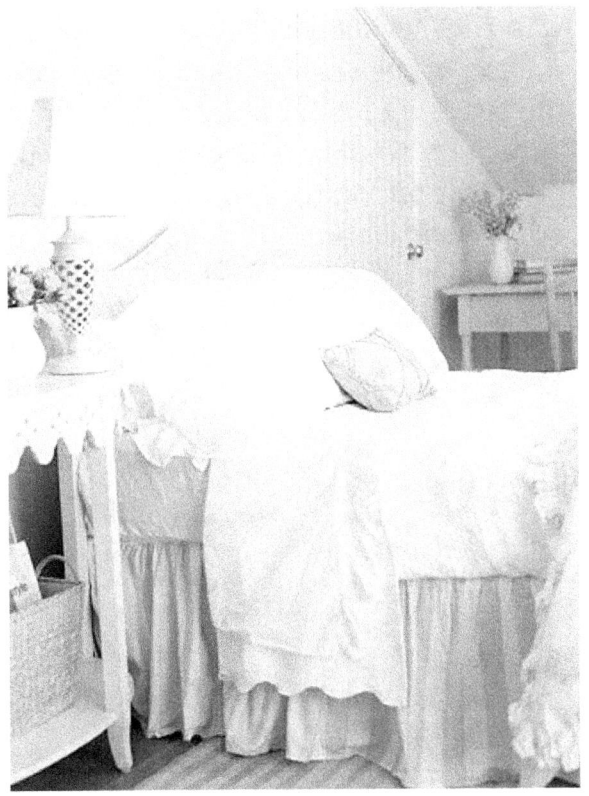

Limit your bed size to a queen unless you have a really large space. Using apartment size furnishings or scaling down the number of pieces in the room will make a dramatic difference in how your room feels.

Paint if possible and visit <u>Chapter 4</u> '<u>Color Your World</u>' to find the color and shade that provides the look and feel you want in your private space. Add texture with rugs, window coverings (hang from the top of the wall rather than the top of the window to make the space feel much larger) throw pillows and plants and top it off with bedding that compliments your other selections.

Take a good look at the living room space and the bedroom space and see which best supports a small computer armoire to create your home office.

Your living area will benefit from a TV that hangs on the wall or a narrow media cabinet that increases storage if you do not add the computer armoire.

You may want to explore adding an apartment size sectional sofa. These can create a break from the dining room and living room and still provide an open and spacious feeling while adding seating.

Cottages and Bungalows are actually smaller versions of a typical home. Space planning is more important than ever to achieve a homey, un-cramped feeling.

Eliminate clutter wherever you are able to; clutter is the chief offender of small spaces.

Cottages or Bungalows

Simple, smooth lines will benefit the feeling of spaciousness in your cottage. Sometimes the mere thought of a 'cottage or bungalow' conjures a vision of a Victorian space complete with curly cues on the lamps and curtains replacing cabinet doors. Lose that image!

Cottages benefit from the Seaside and Country Cottage designs that combine soft colors, upholstered furnishings with clean lines and double duty tables in the living room and dining areas.

All of the ideas presented in the 'Dorm Room' sections apply in small spaces. Visit the Efficiency Apartments section to enhance those ides to cover dining and kitchen solutions.

Most of all enjoy the homey and comfortable atmosphere that is gained from a small space! It makes a large statement if you capture the charm and make it yours.

Chapter 9
And All across the Kingdom!

something for everyone

All across the kingdom describes every space that was not covered in Chapter 8!

If this chapter applies to you, then you probably live in a single family or spacious duplex home or condo that offers more opportunity to expand and enjoy decorating your home and making it perfect for your lifestyle.

All of the challenges regarding using space wisely apply to you as well.

Chapter 5 Chaos is King applies to every home and is worth examining how and where it may exist in yours.

Your challenges may well come from too many walls in places where you need more space, small closets that don't accommodate your lifestyle and the inability to place your furniture into a design that makes the space work for you.

All of these challenges are addressed individually as we move through the next few chapters.

Every solution applies to all of us if we do not readily achieve the results we are looking for. Once we identify our challenges we are able to put the solutions we choose for our homes in place.

Now we're ready to get to the heart of 'Make It Mine!' And remember, everything is possible!

Chapter 10
Beginning To See the Light

see your room in a whole new light

What's YOUR style? You are likely to find it in your lighting selections! This may surprise you but; the light choices you make typically define your style.

Lighting is everything! Choose wisely and you will be well on your way to creating YOUR space. If you are uncertain as to what your style actually is take a look at the lighting examples in this chapter.

Notice what you are drawn to and then explore that look. You will probably find that some of your furniture pieces will work nicely to create that style, the other pieces we will work on!

If you discover that you are drawn to a particular style of lighting, you will probably discover that is your style!

Some are combined styles that work well together to create a specific look and feel.

Great lighting is found in yard sales, online stores, (Overstocked.com is a good one) eBay, and on Craig's List (many contractors sell lighting that customers rejected on Craig's List), in the newspaper, at thrift stores and, especially at the Habitat for Humanity Thrift Store!

Habitat for Humanity has been very blessed to receive donations from Lowes, Home Depot and a host of other large companies. If you have one locally, find it and bookmark it in your mind!

Define Your Style!

Art Deco Lighting

Classical Lighting

Contemporary Lighting

Country Lighting

Country Cottage Lighting

Eclectic Lighting

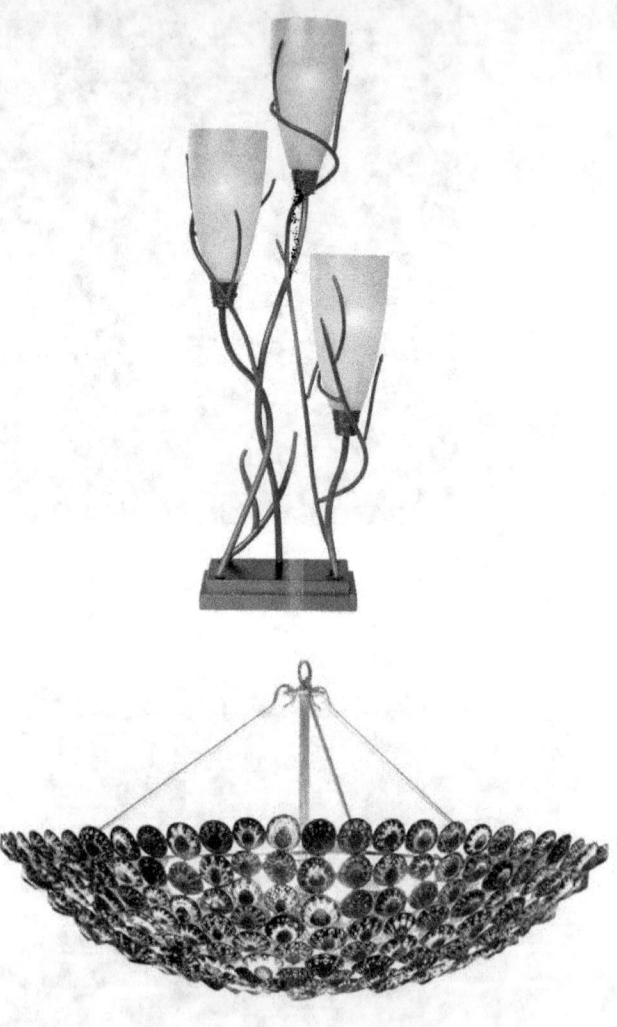

French Country Lighting

Mediterranean Lighting

Minimalist Lighting

Modern Lighting

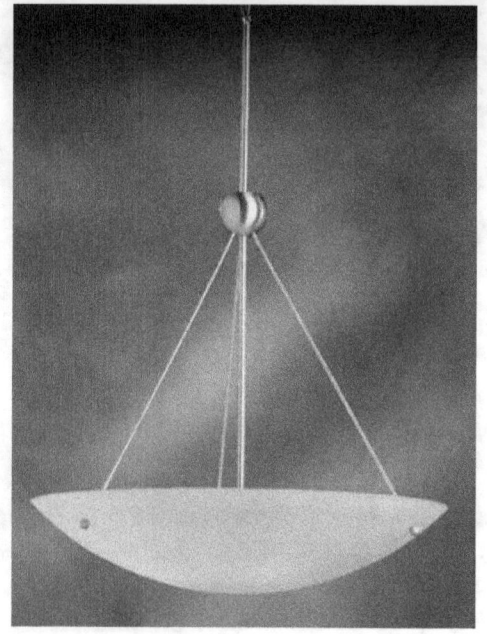

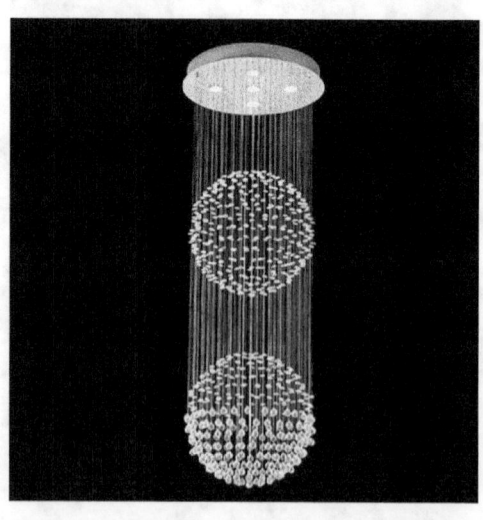

Oriental Lighting

Primitive Lighting

Rustic Lighting

Retro Lighting

Seaside Cottage Lighting

Shabby Chic Lighting

Southwestern Lighting

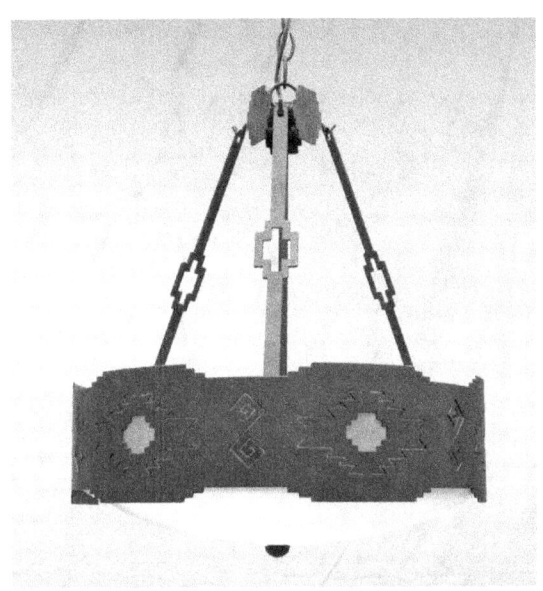

Spanish Lighting

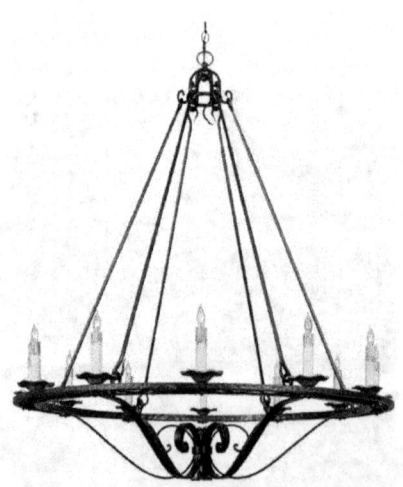

Traditional Lighting

Tuscan Lighting

Victorian Lighting

Whimsical Lighting

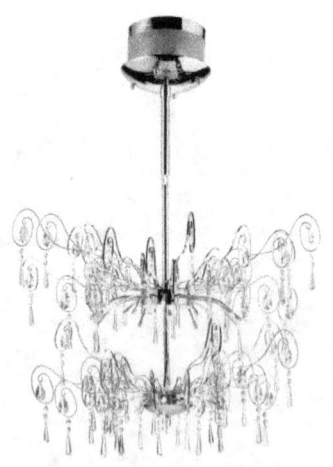

If you take a moment to carefully review the styles you will notice that each has lines, shapes and detail that are particular to the style.

Find the one that you like the most things about the look and feel, imagine them in your own home and you will have defined your own personal style!

Some tips about lighting your palace:

1) Entry areas greet everyone; choose a size in your style that is befitting of the greeting and the size of the area you are defining.

2) **Long entry halls** may require a larger light and wall sconces or an entry table with lamps to properly light the area.

3) **Don't select long, pendant lighting for the entry if you have 8' ceilings.** You can do this in the dining area because the table is placed under the lighting and no one is walking in the area.

4) **Grand foyers deserve a grand light!** Go big or go home.

5) **Wall sconces around mirrors in bath areas are welcoming** and provided necessary dressing light.

6) **Choose your dining room light in proportion with the size of your table.** Don't be afraid to drop it lower than what you might think is typical. Lighting makes a statement! If you want it to be intimate lighting you have to set the stage with furniture and accessories and say it with light!

7) **Avoid fans on dining room lighting** unless you want to create a very informal space. It also cools the food on the table and stirs dust above and onto the food.

8) **Ceiling fans are a must in some areas;** although some decorators rush to remove them, others will scurry to install them! If you determine that a ceiling fan must be in your bedrooms, avoid the inexpensive (and cheap looking) light kits; opt for nice lamps and a decorative fan that matches the room decor.

9) If you have a budget that permits you to **shop for quality fans with lighting that makes a difference in the room**, go for it!

10) Breakfast bars in kitchens become a special place if they are defined with two or **three pendant** lights.

11) **Hall lighting** is largely ignored, yet it is typically a long area that leads to

probably half of your home. Use that opportunity to make a special statement!

Track lighting is now available in attractive styles that fit any décor. You may want to look at those as an option, or, supplement your overhead lights with wall sconces.

Chapter 11
Every Step You Take...

flair for your feet

Floors are important! They are a bit of a roadway as they carry the traffic through your home. Who knew!

After spending all that time on painting and properly defining your home with perfect lighting; there's the same old floor! Now what?

Floors will shout or whisper, depending on how you treat them. Some styles seem to feel like they must be defined by specific flooring. That is the shouting method!

If your floors do not 'match' your idea of the design you are creating you have a few choices to make them whisper so the bulk of your masterpiece will shout.

If you live in an apartment or a rental home you may think you are stuck with your floors; take heart.

Solutions for shouters:

a) **Cover the floor!** That's right; cover it with something that ties it to the style you are creating. Even if the floor has carpet, cover it with a large room size rug or one that leaves only a border of the original color, if there is anything you like about it.

I urge you to check out Flea Markets, Thrift Stores, Consignment Stores, Craig's List and Overstocked.com to find a rug that will make the cut.

b) **Select the very inexpensive woven mats** to create an oriental feeling in the space.

c) **Tile and carpet squares** are sold by the box pretty inexpensively. Find the nap and color that you work for your idea and put them in place.

d) **If you own your home**, have carpet and cannot afford to replace it with anything; take it up and paint the subflooring! It works great with rugs to complete the design.

e) **If you have wood floors** that are the wrong color or in a bad state of repair; make the repairs and rent a floor sander.

Sanding is a fairly easy job that provides you with a clean slate. Then select the stain that makes you want to shout about it!

f) **Barter the work** with someone who has materials and experience.

g) **Create visual points** to break an open floor plan by changing the flooring. In very open plans the entry can break away from tile or something durable to wood or carpet in the actual living space, thereby creating a defined space without walls.

h) **Avoid the 'checkerboard' floor syndrome**. Breaking the flooring is fine for obvious areas like entry's, kitchens, baths and lanais. A different floor color or style in every room dates your home and makes it look and feel choppy and smaller.

When flooring changes design, color or material in every room you will soon begin to feel like you've been check-mated instead of mated with your dream home!

Kicking your old floor to the curb?

Consider other options. If you have always wanted wood floors and they are not practical for your home or location; search out the new tile selections.

Ceramic 'wood look' floor

'Looks like wood' tile floors

Tile manufactures have listened to their buying audience and created beautiful tiles that look like wood. It is easy care, scuff proof and humidity does not affect its performance.

Save diagonal ceramic or marble tile jobs for large rooms. While they are beautiful, they also attract attention to the floor space and make the room appear smaller.

Select light tile colors to make your room appear larger. Larger tile sizes also make the room appear more spacious.

Pergo or other manufactured wood flooring is far less expensive but also, far less durable. It is manmade wood and a little easier to install but have a care here, if it is not properly adhered to the subflooring, it 'bounces' when you walk across it and screams 'thrift.'

Real hard wood is more expensive but if time is on your side you can watch for the spring specials and the dead of winter liquidation of these materials.

Carpeting is still considered a good option for bedrooms and upper levels. It is available in a multitude of styles, naps, colors and designs.

Unless you plan to live forever in your home, or don't mind repainting later, avoid fads and colors that you will tire of. Select colors that you can interchange accessories with to create a new look and feel later.

The general rule with carpeting is Berbers are more durable, neutrals are preferable.

Lose the notion that a carpeted kitchen, bath or dining room is a good idea. Most people prefer to be able to easily clean the surfaces of these areas.

In homes that offer large, separate dining areas this rule can be bent; personally, I'd rather not; opt for wood or tile.

When you begin to install flooring, doors, hardware or plumbing you must decide whether you are handy and want to learn or tackle these tasks alone or, whether it is time to search the kingdom for qualified and affordable assistance.

If so, head to the **'Know When to Fold Em'** chapter and review the section about contractors and subs. This is an area where cutting corners has definite rules of procedure. What's it all about? It is about doing what you can, where you can to claim your space and make it work for you!

Chapter 12
I'm Looking Through You...

create a room with a view

You guessed it; it's time for windows and how to treat them to compliment your plan.

Some window styles reflect the style of the home. For instance, a home with arched windows may be somewhat of a challenge when creating a Primitive Design.

Likewise, the older more typical square windows challenge the Contemporary, Spanish and Southwestern designs.

Once you have selected your style, paint colors and floor treatment, the windows complete your canvas. The picture will be complete when the room is finished!

Tips to begin:

a) **Wash the windows!**

b) **Clean the woodwork and paint** if necessary.

c) **Assess the challenge!** Do the size and style of the windows work as they are, or do you need to change the perception to create your style?

d) **Get creative;** packaged window treatments are made for the 'house of commons,' not your palace! When creating your own design, you become the leader, not the follower.

e) **Measure the actual windows** both vertical and horizontal; then measure from the top of the wall to the floor.

f) **Take a moment and caulk your windows**. Heat and air conditioning is lost through windows and doors, increasing your energy bills and making it harder to heat or cool your home. Caulking also prevents ants and other undesirables from entering your home.

g) **If you live in a manufactured house**, tear down those 'made for a trailer' window treatments! Nothing says I'm perched on wheels like the little valances and kitchen curtains hanging all over the house. You will be amazed at how your home can look!

Now we're ready to begin! Let's look at materials, and what is possible.

If you are working with Southwestern, Spanish or Primitive designs, regardless of whether you have square, arched or small windows; try picking up full length wood bi-fold doors and painting them or grab a can of Min Wax spray stain and put the finish of your choice on the doors. They fold out just like shutters and can be used on sliders as well as windows.

For very little money you have custom window treatments!

Cottage designs work great with the plantation shutter styles. You can hang these higher and wider that the actual window if you need to visually increase the size of the window to make a bigger statement.

Give some thought to hand railing for stairs and how they can work as curtain rods! These come in nearly every style, some with intricate design in addition to the more typical styles.

Mediterranean and Spanish styles can use wrought iron pieces to create interesting rods.

All of these items can be picked up at the same thrift stores, consignment stores, Craig's List and any other source you know would be worth looking at in your area.

We're creating a masterpiece here and can hardly be bothered to simply pick up a simple rod and hang it up. Window design starts from the rods.

If your home has small, older windows try hanging your drapes from the top of the wall and extend them out past the actual window. Visually the wall and the windows appear larger; and the room feels more substantial.

Drop in at the remnant section of the fabric store. Look for large bolts that are offered at $1.00 a yard. You're looking for texture that will compliment your personal style.

If you're not handy with a sewing machine, never fear; just purchase Stitch Witchery and head for your ironing board to create rod pockets at the top and finished hems at the bottom.

Curtains that pool onto the floor are much more appealing and do not look like pre-packaged curtains.

Look at sheets if you do not want to spend time at the fabric store. They are long, offered in a wide range of colors and already have top and bottom hems.

Just slit the sides of the top hem and insert the rod after using your stitch witchery magic or hand needle and thread to complete the newly cut seam.

Sheets work great as shower curtains on spring rods; insert a liner behind it and decorate away!

If you plan to tie your curtains back look at wide cloth ribbon and other trims that are not so fussy and do not appear prepackaged.

If you are working with a Victorian, Classic or Traditional design look at the long table cloths that also offer special designs particular to your style. Try adding long strings of pearls that are found in craft stores and Christmas decorations. They make fabulous trims!

Natural hemp ropes work perfectly as tiebacks for Cottage (especially Seaside Cottage designs) Country and Primitive.

Look for natural fabrics like unbleached muslin to bring a true country or Primitive feeling into the space.

If you have typical windows and are looking for a whole new look with an unconditional fix; define your style and consider adding plantation shutters that are 18" shy of the top of the window.

Next, look for leaded glass or designed to mimic lead stained Plexiglas sections; place this section above the shutter to cover the rest of the window and add a trim board. Suddenly your 'same old windows' now feature leaded glass and thick, rich wood shutters. Stain or paint the shutters to match your design plan.

You no longer have average or typical windows. It's a brand new view!

Avoid those 'found in every home' mini blinds if possible. They feel like a cheap fix, and are unbecoming to a palace and your plan. Dare to be different.

The 'fan' treatment for the top of arched windows needs to head to the curb too. The arches grace the top of the window; leave them bare and let the sun shine in!

Part of the "Make It Mine' plan is to make your home different and spectacular; affordably!

Make a real effort to think outside the traditional prepackaged window treatments available almost everywhere. Search for great deals on things that can be repurposed into your plan.

Chapter 13
Where's the Beef?

This is a figurative and literal complaint with tenants and homeowners alike. The kitchen is the most used room in the house and wear and tear is evident on cabinetry, countertops, walls and floors.

It also appears as the most substantial room in the house; it is designed to do so. Other rooms have walls, windows, a floor and perhaps a door.

Your kitchen comes equipped with walls covered in cabinetry, appliances and a design you did not choose unless you designed the home or remodeled it to your taste.

Let's assume you didn't. Remodeling your kitchen is an expensive proposition.

Homeowners dream about it and plan for it; tenants attempt to shrug it off, believing there is nothing they can do about it.

Worse, many people assume their own style in a home is defined by the cabinetry.

If you are a homeowner review these potential solutions for

Cabinetry:

Painted cabinets in a south Florida home.

Wood trim boards added to 2 kinds of cabinetry before painting

Before and after photos of painted
cabinetry (Slightly different angle)

a) **The most obvious fix is painting**
the cabinets. If this is the choice you are
making you may be surprised at the
myriad of paint treatments available.

Study them carefully and choose one that fits your new design plan. These pictures represent a before and after preview of a kitchen. The angles are different but you can easily see they are the same kitchen.

This couple opted for changing out the hardware and adding updated appliances; their completed design plan appeared to be a brand new kitchen. The savings on this room alone were $29,000.00.

b) To get a good finish that you will be proud of, plan on **removing all the cabinet doors** and hardware.

c) **The hardware can be sprayed** in a color or finish that compliments your cabinet paint selection.

d) If your cabinets are wood you can **rent a small hand sander and rough up the existing finish** and smooth out any blemishes.

e) **If your cabinets are plastic** coated (this is another shocker, a lot of the newer cabinets are coated with plastic to appear wood) look for the application that will adhere to the smooth finish allowing your paint to adhere to the current finish.

f) **Primitive and Country designs** look great with the bases painted a dark or neutral color; then add barn siding with adhesive and change out the hardware to match.

g) **Cottage designs** work perfectly with the bases painted white and bead board adhered to the doors.

h) **Southwestern designs** look great with the spray on treatment that looks like sandstone. Just apply and then spray the poly as a top coat.

i) **Budget permitting**, you can purchase new doors and finish them with a stain or Min Wax. You will need to sand the bases and apply the same stain treatment or purchase the covers for the bases when you buy the doors.

This process will produce an entirely new kitchen when it is completed.

If you are ready to tear out walls and redesign the kitchen; that's another book.

If you have the space, look for a table with drawers, a buffet that is substantial or prep table and paint it a contrasting color to create an island.

Add wood or Plexiglas chopping blocks across the section you want to use for food prep and dramatically increase your counter space.

Take a look at the trim pieces that Lowe's and Home depot feature.

Cabinets should be arranged so that glasses, coffee cups and the items most used are around the sink area.

Plates, serving bowls and other place setting dishes and the larger bowls used for food preparation should be near the stove.

The base cabinets should be used for canned goods, each placed near the area where you keep the proper bowls to prepare or serve the items.

Small appliances and pans should be stored in the base cabinets near the area where they will be used.

The ideal kitchen sports a triangle layout with the sink at mid point, the range and refrigerator across from the sink to complete the triangle layout. This is a step saving and time saving layout.

Your 'Plain Jane' cabinets become rich, new and can even appear Tuscan by adding the corner trim pieces to the base of your cabinet corners and the edges of your upper cabinetry.

They appear to be deep and thick but actually adhere to and wrap the corners of the cabinets; this completely alters the appearance of the cabinets making them appear far more substantial.

Purchase the trim pieces that extend to the floor for Tuscan, Spanish and Mediterranean designs.

The wood is intricately carved or super simple; choose the one that works with your design plan.

Matching decorative trim pieces can be used to replace the tiny one inch trim at the tops of the cabinets.

Trims To Change Your Style

a) Take a long, close look at the toe kickboards (the trim at the bottom of the cabinets by the floor). If yours are wood, paint or touch up the stain if they are scuffed.

b) If your kitchen cabinets are finished with the rubber trim that has been used for many years in less expensive cabinetry, tear it off and replace it.

c) Home improvement stores all offer this very affordably. Pick up a can of adhesive while you're there. You need it in your 'tool kit!'

d) You must have your own tool kit!

e) If you have more than ample base cabinet space think about leaving the doors and hardware off of one set of strategically placed base cabinets; fill the screw holes with wood filler, sand and paint or stain to match the cabinets and add decorative baskets that hold vegetables and fruit.

f) This also works if you have located that perfect accessory table to use as an island (one with a shelf). Look for baskets or containers that compliment your style.

g) This is a space and time saver, providing easy access for food preparation.

h) If you have open wall space that does not offer anything you are interested in using consider this option to add storage and interest to that area.

Check your favorite thrift stores and Craig's List for a hutch that compliments or contrasts with your kitchen design.

Another storage solution

Anchor the hutch to the wall with screws and add trim boards that match your kitchen trim. Presto! You have a gorgeous new addition to your kitchen. The one pictured above was offered for $50.00 on Craig's List!

This is another style of older hutch that can be anchored to the wall and painted a contrasting color to give your kitchen an entirely new look and feel while adding storage!

My best result with this was an older dark wood hutch with straight lines and glass doors. I used touchup pens and polished it. It became the showpiece of the kitchen!

Adding an eating area:

If you have a 'breakfast nook' or eat in kitchen consider using a contrasting or matching base cabinetry as your table base by simply adding a piece of glass to the top.

This also works with pieces of furniture such as accent tables if they are the correct height. If you can imagine it, you can make it happen!

Find seating that compliments your design and works for your family at thrift stores.

Adding an office area to your kitchen:

If you have extra wall space in your kitchen, usually near a corner, and need a computer workspace or small office; look for base cabinet drawers or upper cabinets that add a look you want in your kitchen.

Measure the height! Too low is a back breaker and too high will make your arms so tired you never want to come back.

Place one cabinet at each end of the space and anchor them to the wall.

Call local cabinet installers and granite shops and ask about remnant pieces and go out to check them out. They can cut it down for you to fit your space; granite remnants are available in the $100.00 price range.

Use adhesive to anchor the top to the bases.

If granite is not your style, look for glass pieces or narrow table tops that can be disconnected from the legs and anchor the top to the cabinets.

If your desktop is long enough, look for matching or contrasting upper cabinets and anchor them at each end to complete your private office with loads of storage.

If not, look for the compartmentalized shelving units typically used for display and anchor them to the wall above to maximize the use of space and increase storage!

Countertops:

Countertops are at the top of the list of things people hate about their kitchens. They are either worn, burned, dated or just plain ugly.

Consider the following solutions; if these do not seem feasible you may at least have expanded your idea of what changes can be completed easily. If so, apply a fix that feels right to you.

a) **Solid surface and granite countertops** are the most desirable. If you have them, we will be covering how to treat them in later chapters.

Granite Countertops

If you want them, then spend some time pricing and budgeting for the installation.

As a rule of thumb; light cabinetry goes will with darker surface countertops; dark cabinetry is compliment by lighter surface countertops.

The exception to this rule is when you want to create a white on white kitchen.

White granite is rare and expensive but there are solid surface solutions that work nicely.

If you are planning a complete remodel of your kitchen all of the tips and pitfalls, including pricing and arrangement, will be featured in the remodeling version of 'Make It Mine', available in the near future.

b) **Formica** is glued onto plywood to create your countertops. The Formica can be removed and replaced with a new color and design that compliments your style.

Just measure and head back to your favorite online search engine and look for the best pricing. The adhesive is sold at hardware and home improvement stores, typically the same stores that offer the Formica.

Formica Countertops

c) **Stainless steel** is sold in rolls. If this is your choice, use adhesive to attach it to the wood that is exposed from removing the Formica.

If you choose not to remove the Formica, you must sand the existing Formica countertop before applying adhesive. If you fail to do this it will pop up in the heated kitchen and become a dismal failure.

Stainless Countertops

d) Strip off the old Formica and install a **tile** that makes your statement. If you use tile don't leave off the sealer coat when you are finished.

If you fail to follow this advice you will soon notice grout that lifts and falls out or changes color, giving your new countertop a completely different look.

Tile Countertops

e) **Tiling a countertop** is not a new idea; however, you can also use 20" pieces of marble and install exactly as the tile is installed.

Pick a complimentary grout color, seal and you have marble countertops.

f) Contemporary and a few other design styles work well with **concrete countertops**.

Concrete Countertops

While this is more typical for lofts and very contemporary spaces, concrete comes in colors now and a whole new set of design ideas spring from that change. This also requires a sealant.

g) **Whimsical designs and cottages** work nicely with mosaic tiles on the countertops. Again, peel the Formica off and then buy scraps of colored tiles that match your décor.

Mosaic Tile Countertops

Break the tile pieces with a hammer (cover tile with plastic and wear goggles when you break the tiles). Lightly sand the rough edges. These pieces can be randomly placed and glued onto the Formica, if it is sanded first to create a rough surface for the glue to adhere to.

Finish with a complimentary grout color. This process is less expensive due to the opportunity to purchase remnants of tiles rather than a large group of matching tiles.

Mismatched appliances draw attention to, and age the entire look of the kitchen. Appliance spray paint is inexpensive and the easiest way to match the appliances.

If you are feeling particularly creative you can purchase sheets of stainless coating with peel off backs. Remove handles and anything that protrudes and use a box cutter to cut the sheets to the proper size. Finally, peel off the back and apply carefully, avoiding pressing unwanted seams onto your 'new' appliance.

Or, budget permitting head back to your favorite new shopping spots to **steal good deals** and to pick up appliances that are well loved and slightly used. My best bargains come from Craig's List; which is probably obvious by this point!

Many builders remove these packages from model homes and offer them on Craig's List.

If your refrigerator currently looks like a scrap book think about moving the catch all magnets and pictures to the side; or purchase an inexpensive small bulletin board and frame those 'special' pieces to really showcase them

Faux Stainless covered
Range and Refrigerator

Fixtures:

Lowes and Home depot offer repair kits for porcelain sinks that can make yours appear new.

They also offer plastic sinks that are very pretty and appear porcelain and are heavy duty. I found this shocking the first time I discovered these! The prices, styles and overall look will amaze you. It's not nearly as big an issue as it appears to be.

Last but not least, head to Habitat for Humanity Thrift Store, yard sales, the trusty Craig's List and call local plumbers to see if they have what you need in their back room.

They store the sinks that customers refuse in their back room. You can get a great price from them.

Faucets speak volumes about kitchens. Try all of the above to locate one that does not break your budget and compliments your kitchen. It is the finishing touch. I much prefer repairing or picking up a vintage faucet in lieu of a $20.00 wanna be faucet found in every discount department store.

From blight to a beautiful sight:

If you have a kitchen from the late 70's and 80's that features a ceiling that is intended to mimic a 'cove' ceiling graced by florescent lights hidden behind Plexiglas pieces like the one depicted below, you should be more than ready for a change.

These kitchens do not have a soffit (the drywall above the cabinets) as this is replaced by the lighting design.

If your budget does not accommodate a complete change or you do not have help to tear it out; or, even if your are renting, give some thought to taking down the Plexiglas and covering it with decorative film that matches or compliments your theme.

A rental will require prior permission or your willingness to replace the dreaded Plexiglas with new when you leave.

I am willing to bet the owner will much prefer your look to their previous look so fear not!

You can also use spray paint designed to cover plastic and get rid of those ugly tracks that define and hold the sections of Plexiglas.

This is a beautiful fix to affordably update a really dated idea. Make sure to purchase the transparent version of the film; it is offered in several varieties.

Otherwise you will be looking for your light through a dark cover. This is amazingly affordable!

The film covers pictured here are just a sample of what is available. You can use your search engine to look at the many styles offered.

Online shopping will bring them straight to your door. If you prefer an up close and personal approach head to the nearest Lowes or local home improvement store.

Faux Tray Ceilings created with Plexiglas and Florescent Lighting.

Film Coverings for Cove Lighting

Backsplashes:

Every kitchen needs a backsplash! They protect the walls from grease damage and provide the perfect opportunity to give your kitchen a final treatment that projects your style and design.

Tile is the most common backsplash. It is durable, comes in many sizes, shapes and designs and lasts a lifetime if maintained properly.

If you have granite countertops you will typically have marble tiles to match.

Marble Tiled backsplash

This kind of backsplash is beautiful with any kind of countertop; however, it is an expensive solution.

The simplest tiled backsplash for a novice to install is the 1 inch squares that come with on a 12 x 12 inch mat. Still, you must be prepared to cut tile.

1" Glass block tile backsplash

A side grinder is a handheld tool that is capable of performing most tile cuts simply. If you're thinking of the cumbersome wet saws for this job I encourage you to try this first. It is one of those miraculous tips you never want to forget!

Let's examine a few others; Take a good look at the following pictures, notice the 'look and feel' that each backsplash inspires in you.

This is a good test to see how it will make anyone who enters the room feel. Some feel commercial and busy, some cozy and some simply beautiful! Find the one that suits your personal taste.

Subway and 16" ceramic tile

Hammered tin backsplash

Hammered tin is a quick, decorative and inexpensive fix that can be anchored to the wall and removed when leaving if you are renting your home.

Now you are ready to tackle the windows, flooring and change out overhead and under cabinet lighting with all the tricks of trade we've covered in the previous chapters.

If you are a tenant and the cabinetry is worn you may be able to negotiate a part of your rent to upgrade and make the above changes.

If you are in an apartment community you will probably find that impossible.

But, there is always a way, since 'no does not mean no' you can take down the lighting and fans, remove the hardware and faucets and pack them away in a box and replace with your own. Then add the 'island', space permitting.

I have never, ever moved into a rental property without painting and changing out these items. And, I have never regretted it!

When it is time to move, reverse the process; and head to Craig's List and post a free ad to become a seller instead of a purchaser for any items you no longer need.

Now, the only beef in your kitchen is being served in your beautifully redesigned dining area!

Chapter 14
Splish, Splash,
Time for the Bath!

retreat. refresh. revive.

Baths are next in line for design repair; this is due mostly to the volume of use, wear and tear they must endure.

Baths appear tired because they are tired.

Declining value in a home begins in the kitchen and baths; rendering them the biggest culprit in making homes appear old and in a bad state of repair.

Worse still, the design of the bathroom will place you squarely into the vintage time and place it was built. Why?

Even bath designs have changed dramatically over time. Every 10 years or so, a dramatic new design is introduced.

Walk into a bathroom in a home built before 1950 and you will find a small room with a low bathtub that doubles as a shower, a pedestal sink, tile that ranges from very small 1" tiles to black and white checks on the floor and walls, a commode in front of a window and a wall space to add a free standing cabinet for the bath linens. A second one half bath is usually found 'off the kitchen.'

Walk into a new home built in 2011 and be prepared to be impressed!

The 'master bath' is now the same size as former bedrooms; showers are separate from the roman soaking tub and frequently sport triple or quadruple shower heads and a seat to use while enjoying your shower.

Commodes are much taller and fit for a king (the proverbial throne). They have heated seats, auto flush mechanisms and even a storage in the tank for cleaning chemicals that are, of course, auto dispensed.

Better still, a bidet is perched alongside and both are front and center in their own private room, with a door.

Tile in baths in 2011 range from none except for shower and tub (wet) areas to showers that have travertine marble walls and ceilings!

Long cabinets, much taller (42") than their counterparts from years gone by, line the walls to create a 'his and her space.'

Windows are almost never found near a tub in 2011. Many times windows are located high on the walls to allow natural light to penetrate the room while maintaining privacy.

Skylights still dominate large baths for natural lighting and maximum privacy.

Today's baths have large closets built-in, to house a multitude of linens and provide storage for a 'spa' look and feel in your private space.

It is about intimate time for revitalization.

Your bath need not look like a 2011 bath. It also need not look like a 1950 bath. Our goal is to allow your style and budget to merge with the materials at hand; showcasing them as the very best they can be!

Let's aim for creating a bath that features the things most important to you. Start with the simple and easy things you can change.

a) **If your walls are covered in tile** half way up on most or every wall, remove it or paint it a color that works for your design.

Epoxy paint will cover the glass tile, remain adhered to the tile and completely alter the look of your bath.

Removing the tile in all areas except the shower/bath area will update your space dramatically and alter the time capsule you are stuck in. This will require scraping the adhesive that anchored the tile, sanding and probably some slight drywall repair that anyone can complete.

In later chapters we will review time and money saving tips and little tricks for completing the simpler, big jobs.

b) **Pedestal sinks are a perfect fit for half baths,** not so much for master or large guest baths. They offer zero storage, no counter tops and basically just sit there and allow water to pour through.

These sinks are perfect in a half bath; they save space in addition to appearing very sturdy and substantial. Most people associate pedestal sinks with an earlier period in design styles.

c) **If your tub is less than your ideal** and a replacement is out of the question; look closely at the condition of the tub.

Older tubs are nearly always porcelain, which is fairly easy to patch. The kits are sold at most home improvement stores.

If you have a tub that is constructed from one of the new plastics; you probably never dreamed that it was! Repair kits for these mainly consist of a polymer patch and paint.

The most common complaint about tubs, disregarding the low height, is the buildup of lime and other minerals that have turned the tub either a rusty orange or the grayish lime deposit color.

Even if these appear to be unconquerable; you can wage war against mineral deposits with CLR and Lime Away among other products.

Both of these products are very strong, and have serious warnings for proper usage as do all chemicals. Heed them.

Sometimes harsh chemicals are necessary; they still present a very serious risk when used without the precautionary instructions.

If chemicals are impossible for you to use, take a good look at the citrus or steam cleaning products. The progress may be slower but the benefit is found in the lack of dangerous chemicals. You may have to scrape or use an abrasive pad but, remember tile is glass and porcelain will scratch. Tread carefully with any kind of scraping as a misstep will damage the tile.

In most instances you will be able to remove all of the mineral deposits and shine the tub, faucet, drain and tiles.

I always try this first, and then decide what next step to take regarding the tub and shower area.

If you are interested in trying very long fabric, drapes or sheets for your shower curtain (2 simple and inexpensive spring tension rods lets you easily determine the height for both the cloth curtain and a very inexpensive liner) you will pretty much be able to disregard the tile's effect on your design once it is cleaned.

Stainless steel inserts are now available. These are screwed into the drywall or a strong adhesive is used to apply to the wall surface.

Take a look at the new 'looks like tile' insets! Gone are the cheap plastic walls that bent in when you leaned against them! The new inserts come in an array of colors and designs and anyone would be proud to show them off in their new design plan. They are much less expensive then purchasing tile and having it installed and easier to maintain

'Looks like tile' shower insert.

Combine this with the floor tile (pictured) that looks like wood and imagine what you can create!

A little imagination and the willingness to roll up your sleeves or ask friends to help and you will have a 'new bath' pretty easily!

'Looks like wood tile floors'

If you have built in vanities in your current bath and the space is sufficient for your plan, review the cabinetry section of our kitchen makeovers.

Many solutions are covered in that section including painting the original cabinets

It pays off in a big way to jump in and add your own ideas. This method produces the same results in a bath area.

The kitchen cabinetry section offers many other ideas to consider; the effect is the same in the kitchen or bath for cabinetry.

Don't be afraid to try some of these methods. The biggest complaint about painted cabinetry is the RUNS!

If your paint runs, use a very fine grain piece of sand paper and take out the run, wipe off the sanding grit and repaint. Pick up a couple of cans of spray poly in the paint department. This will add a hard, shiny finish that can withstand water splashes and washing.

If you do not have the cabinetry you need, head back to the thrift shopping spots, Habitat for Humanity thrift store and Craig's List where nearly new cabinets can be found at ridiculously inexpensive prices.

The down side of this is the install. If you can handle either hiring someone or doing it yourself, go for it!

If you have a flat mirror anchored over your sink with little screws in plastic caps... tear down that mirror! Normally four screws will anchor the mirror.

Plan on a minor wall repair with your can of patch; let it dry and lightly sand and paint with your wall color.

Decorative mirrors can be found everywhere for every budget. If you have a double sink, hang one above each sink and add wall sconces to properly light the area and complete your design.

If removing the mirror is not possible due to budget concerns or you're living in a rental, think about a Plan B:

Measure the existing mirrors entire surface and hunt down a picture frame in that size or look for thin wood in the desired width and frame your mirror.

Trim is available in every style at your local Lowes or Home Depot stores. The edges will require being mitered which is a little tricky.

Many times I have managed to get the workers at Lowes to make the cuts for me. You MUST be sure of your sizes because if they are wrong, you cannot return the pieces for a refund.

In addition to the countertop tips in the kitchen section, I have many times managed to secure a piece of remnant granite for bathrooms for $100.00. The supplier will also cut the opening if you ask.

This is a perfect time to search for a vessel sink. These sit on top of the countertop with only a small opening for the plumbing.

Vessel Sinks

A $100.00 piece of granite with vessel sink

You can also look around your home or in our thrift suggestions and find a gorgeous desk or buffet and have the opening cut out for the sink and plumbing.

If you currently have a very low and outdated commode in your bathroom, go back to the Habitat for Humanity Thrift

Store or Craig's list for newly used commodes very, very inexpensively.

If you have decided to keep your current countertop and sink then continue the cleaning process and add your favorite candles or accessories that will instill a feeling of relaxation and rejuvenation.

Commodes are not that expensive when purchased new. If your budget will accommodate one, head back to your favorite home improvement store.

Commodes are amazingly easy to install. They require only a wax ring to seal it and two screws with caps.

Visit the flooring section of 'Make It Mine' for floor solutions. Pay particular attention to the new tile that looks like wood pictured in this chapter.

If possible avoid metal stands that hold tiles and other whatnots and opt for large baskets to hold towels.

Another outdated bath accessory is the little wicker or rattan hanging shelving. You'll have a much richer look if you hang a cabinet or wood shelving unit. Glass shelving is also easy to install and works very nicely with modern, classic and contemporary designs.

Opt for an overhead chandelier if possible to complete your knock out bath!

Chapter 15
Who's that Knocking at My Door?

Your entry area is a vital space in your home. It is the warm greeting that says 'welcome home' to you each day, the place where new friends gain the ever important first impression and also; the place where people who are not welcome are detained or sent packing!

Many apartments and some homes do not offer a designated entry area. This is especially true for the 'open space' concept homes.

If you do not have an entry area, take a look at these suggestions:

Natural   Green

a) **Try placing tall silk bamboo trees on the open side.** These trees provide a natural breaking point to designate the size of the entry and yet, still leave slight openings to continue the open concept. Space will determine how many you will line up.

b) **Open tall shelving units** provide the same visual breaking point as above and allow you to display your accessories very nicely.

c) **An entry table or buffet** will determine the space in your entry. Place a lamp or other accessory that is tall to continue breaking the space. This doubles as a place to add lighting in your smaller entry areas.

d) **If you entry does not have natural light** place a mirror on the wall facing a naturally lighted wall. This will reflect the light back to your entry.

e) **If you entry is long** it is probably darker at the end of it. Try placing wall lighting that travels down the hall and welcomes your guests.

f) **Get rid of clutter** Shoe racks and tables and chairs are a perfect dropping point for anything that is in your hands. A chair is a good idea, space permitting, as it allows you to seat the people who are not friends and keep them out of your private space.

g) **If you live in an area where umbrellas are a necessity**, look for a beautiful tall vase to grace your entry and hold the umbrellas.

Visit the lighting section of this book to review lighting details for the entry. Entertain the idea of adding a dimmer switch to your entry light. You can control the look and feel of any space by adjusting or changing the lighting.

Entry halls are one of the few areas that can still sport soft natural wallpaper designs if desired.

If you elect to wallpaper any wall, prepare it properly so you will be able to remove it if you change design styles in the future. Improperly installed wallpaper can wreak havoc in the removal process and damage walls in a way that may require a professional to repair it.

If you are adding an entry table, keep it simple and narrow to allow traffic to pass through unimpeded.

Avoid those cutsy matching mirror and wall sconces that hold candles. Look for things that complement each other and create your own design on the walls.

Vintage candle sticks or candle wall sconces are available at thrift stores. Add these to grace your mirror or pictures to provide a look that far more attractive.

In every instance, if you decide to add a display to your entry table, display items in odd numbered (3, 5 or 7) groupings. The results will be so much more pleasing to the eye than even numbers (2, 4 or 6). It just is!

Clean the door; paint it if necessary or touchup the stain on the door, both inside and out. Your door is the mirror to your home. Show it off with pride.

Chapter 16

Trading Spaces Working Places

Computers are found in the majority of homes today. We live in a drive thru society that encourages us to hurry up and hurry home.

Laptops with cases that double as a handbag have become as common as the old fashioned change purse that no one left home without.

A PC desktop version typically graces some part of today's home.

Many 'gravy' jobs now offer the opportunity to 'work at home' saving your travel time and your companies' budget for offices. Convenience is everything in our world today.

The parlors of old have given way to the 'home office.'

If you have the opportunity and space to have a home office you know exactly where it should be! If not, it should be as close to the door as possible.

This allows you to keep your business acquaintances separated from your family and personal space. The traffic pattern should be in the door, to your office and out the door and that's the message locating your office by the front door provides. Everyone you do business with is not necessarily your friend.

The best office layout places your desk facing the door. It is uncomfortable and sometimes downright unnerving to face the wall, never knowing who is approaching your space.

In the same way the best chair in a restaurant faces the door, the person controlling the business transacted in an office faces the door.

Space permitting, you should locate a table, credenza or some piece of furniture behind the desk to add lighting and hold printers and fax machines.

If you are attempting to change your office's look and feel, begin with the paint. Chapter 4 'Color Your World' visits how paint sets the tone of a space and what effects colors have on the people in the room.

It is vital to your success to create an atmosphere that will derive the effect on your customers that you are seeking.

Place seating for the visitors to your office at least 2 feet away from and facing the desk. Anything closer is uncomfortable and moves visitors into your personal space.

We all have a comfort zone that extends as far as our outstretched arm extends. When anyone moves closer into that space we begin to feel uncomfortable and even offended.

This also holds true for the spacing of seating in proximity to your desk. This allows you and your visitors to be comfortable and still places you in a control position.

Natural or silk plants work to increase the feeling of comfort in an office setting.

Locate the plants or trees that fit your available space. Never place plants between you and your visitors. It is a visual barrier, uncomfortable and will prevent closing a sales transaction. Anything that impedes a clear visual contact will have this same effect.

If you have business contacts visiting your home office keep the pictures on the walls impersonal. You can place a few family photos on the credenza; however, your office should appear impersonal and prompt a business atmosphere if you expect to be treated in the same manner a business office evokes.

If you need a computer desk in your home and simply do not see a place to call an office, look for a large closet area that you can do without.

You can place two base kitchen cabinets that have drawers, one at each end and add either a piece of remnant granite, glass or wood from a table top to create a built in desk. Add cabinets above for enhanced storage.

You can leave the doors on to close your office off when not in use or take them off and have an open space. If you are living in an apartment with no storage for doors, try sliding them under a bed for safekeeping. Then re-hang them when you leave.

Chapter 17
Barely Get Along Street

Once upon a time, in a very prosperous kingdom, a district was referred to as 'Barely Get Along Street;' the area was filled with homeless, hapless individuals who had not yet learned to be prosperous.

Others in the Kingdom frequently 'threw them a dime' and donated their cast offs to this area. And, so it was that no one wanted to be associated with 'Barely Get Along Street.'

That was then, this is now!

The 'Barely Get Along Street' district has become hip and chic.

The residents in the kingdom wasted many opportunities and fell into the trap of complacency and soon their prosperity was siphoned off, knights lost their commission in the royal palace and a pall fell across the entire kingdom.

Although everyone was affected, the people who knew best how to navigate this state of affairs all seemed familiar with the 'Barely Get Along Street' District.

As they watched their comings and goings much was written about the people

in this area. The perception that they had
no choice was quickly replaced by the
knowledge that they had made a better
choice!

These residents found great value in
the 'stuff' other people tossed without a
thought.

They looked harshly at waste and
pollution of the kingdom and beyond, and
worse still, their homes were just as nice
as the highest family in the royal
hierarchy.

They dressed nicely and had little or
no debt for the collector to come knocking
at their door demanding their hard earned
dollars.

All across the kingdom residents
began to watch how these people
operated in their daily lives; it was the
dawn of a new era!

One where we are all responsible for
our actions and where hands that reached
out were touched in a beautiful way by
people who had never before reached out!

Dumpster divers posted their wares at
a place called Craig's List; and their goods
were very valuable and affordable!

No longer were there cast offs with a
long life time yet to be lived stacked into a

disposal pile. Someone fell in love, again, and the cycle of recycle became the norm.

Thrift stores popped up at every corner of the kingdom, even near the palace. Owners whose efforts were not successful in selling their goods consigned them to a better salesperson.

At every turn in the kingdom the residents were treated with the opportunity to find better quality items at more affordable prices and; to make them theirs! How you may ask?

By repurposing! Everyone's doing it now. We have discarded the idea that new cheap particle board furniture is preferable over used furniture!

The savvy buyer today looks for great quality, sturdy wood and a look and feel they can relate to.

They take it home and change it to fit their own dream home plans and the cycle continues.

Debts were cleared from the books in the kingdom; families began sharing time together repurposing their new finds and laughter once again permeated the kingdom!

This resulted from the diminished stress the residents of the kingdom were feeling, having tossed the notion that they had to 'be' anything accept what they were comfortable being. And life was good again!

The most recognized shopping spots in today's 'Barely Get Along Street' districts are eBay, Goodwill, Salvation Army and Craig's List.

These are quickly joined by Habitat for Humanity Thrift Stores, other thrift stores, consignment stores, yard and garage sales and classifieds in your local newspaper.

Once you see what terrific finds are available you will be inspired to join as a seller to repurpose your pieces that no longer fit.

Ah! There is joy in the kingdom!

A word of caution:
Do not make buying trips to a strangers home or invite strangers to your home for selling items alone.

Ask a friend or neighbor to join you. There is safety in numbers! If you feel anything odd about the transaction use your shoes to win the battle and walk away. 'Gut instinct' has saved many a person from a bad experience!

NEVER send payments by Western Union or any other method to a person you cannot meet or to a place you cannot get to or in.

Discard any ad or response that relates a sad sack story about the person having to leave the country but keys etc. will be mailed to you. They won't.

I avoid any Craig's List ad that does not include a telephone number. I rarely respond to emails. Let them call you. You can make a better judgment on who you are dealing with if you hear their voice and the sincerity as they talk with you.

Don't accept checks or money orders for payments. My youngest son has just given his second vehicle away, complete with title to a stranger who first gave a Postal Money Order and the last time produced a Cashier's Check.

Both were worthless paper. Both are hopeless situations for him. These crimes are rarely solved.

If your buyer is not comfortable bringing all the cash, accept a deposit and let them bring it back when they pick up the item.

Don't set yourself up for a failure, or for unnecessary danger.

If your budget is nearing the bottom of the barrel keep a vigilant watch on the **For Sale 'Free' section of Craig's List.** Many people discard really good pieces by posting a **'Curb Alert".**

These people do not have the time or the inclinations to attempt a sale but are happy to see someone who can use their things take them away. Imagine!

Personally I have never heard of a bad experience with curb alerts. The price tag alone suggests this is a good deal!

When you visit a consignment store, don't hesitate to make an offer; this is especially true if you are making multiple purchases.

Consignment prices should always present a value hoped to attain.

Keep it going! Join the sellers queue and collect the value from your items to add to your decorating budget; or donate the items to worthy resellers.

It's a little like early American barn raisings, where neighbors help neighbors and everyone is a pioneer! Skid Row morphed into Skid Rose (as in rose from the ashes!) And all was well again!

Chapter 18

Let's Give Them
Something to Talk About!

Now that your guests have cleared security at your entry area, lead the way to the 'Living Room'!

I suppose the name was assigned to this room because of the amount of time we plan to spend in it!

What a tall order; to create a room, a single room, where an entire family can live in it.

Let's do it!

First, measure your wall space and make note of window placement. Write it down; sketch a layout of the room, including doors and windows and their proximity to one another!

Before you decide what furniture will be included in this particular masterpiece of a room, think about it!

Make a note about how it will be used in your family, what things are vital and non negotiable and what things can go if there is a pinch for space or design.

Next, decide on a color to set the tone and mood you want to achieve in this space. A quick trip back to Chapter 4 **'Color Your World'** will help you select the perfect color.

Remember there are shades and hues of every color; find the one that best suits you and your family, and your plan. You need only to determine what you want this room to feel like before selecting your color.

Next, decide what the focal point of your room will be. This is typically a fireplace, a great view or some area of the room that will hold the most used items like the TV.

In the living room pictured below, the room had 18 foot ceilings; it was a condo with nothing to define it sitting next door to 119 just like it. We added the fireplace from Lowes for $289.00 and hung a free standing cabinet for display above the fireplace.

The opposite wall was perfect for a very large TV armoire and enclosed bookshelves. This provided two focal points, determined by which way you were facing in the room.

We changed out the fans and chandeliers for replacement fans to suit the owner's décor and added lighting on tables and on the floor.

Seaside Cottage Living Room

The owner selected a seaside cottage look for her home. The carpet flooring was replaced with wood, which was sanded and a white bone finish applied.

If you are blessed with a particularly large living room or a combo living room/family room commonly referred to as a great room; you can combine two points of interest in the space.

This is a good example of an owner who took a look at what she had purchased and set about to make it hers.

The point is, never mind what it appears to be when you start, your goal is to make it work for your family and your design style, affordably.

Find your focal point; then begin arranging your furnishings in a manner that will allow the space to be lived in comfortably while traffic moves freely about the room.

Seating should be grouped around your focal point; it should also be arranged to permit conversations between the people in the room.

Avoid overly large pieces of furniture in an effort to make the space fit the furniture. The objective is to make the furniture comfortable in the space.

This allows for the primary focal point and a secondary point of interest that typically includes a quiet time space to read, a desk or some other special area you want to create in the room.

This area should be at the furthest distance from the hub of activity in the room.

Measure the pieces you intend to keep in the room. If you can locate a roll of painter's tape you will be able to measure the pieces of furniture and place them with the tape to see exactly how the floor space and traffic pattern responds to your ideas.

This saves back breaking labor for plans that simply won't work!

If you are using a TV set as your focal point, place it in an attractive setting such as a wall unit, hanging above a media cabinet or on a media cabinet. In other words, make it earn the cherished position of the focal point of your room.

Display it attractively! Add a plant, tree or other accessory beside the area to further designate it as your focal point. Whatever your plan, execute it with pride.

Place your sofa in the area with the largest blank space open that also allows the people in the room to enjoy the focal point.

Leave at least two feet between sofas, chairs and love seats and the coffee table. Anything less is uncomfortable, feels crowded and causes knee injuries and a painful experience in your home.

Avoid the matching sofa, love seat, chair settings. Choose the sofa as your primary piece and then complement it with different colors or patterns that allow all of the pieces to show off. One matching chair or even a matching love seat can be overcome by adding a contrasting piece to the grouping.

Carefully review the flooring, lighting and window covers sections in this book for ideas on how to arrive at the look you are creating.

Examine the idea of adding a sofa table (even if it is a buffet in disguise that will add valuable space for storage, games, etc. that your family uses. When placed at the back of the sofa or love seat it frees up wall space, adds wood tones and a place to add lighting or candles and display space.

I hope you do not entertain the idea of placing your sofa against the wall, in front of the window. So help me that look is the basis of the 'House of Commons.'

It says, "I did not know what to do with anything so I just pushed it against the white walls and lined everything up!" That is not a 'Make It Mine' warriors plan.

Invest in a set of 'moving coasters.' These are available at Dollar Stores, discount department stores and all home improvement stores. The worst job in arranging a room just became a breeze with these coasters.

Pull pieces into your grouping; leave the walls for spectacular wall hangings and accessories.

Don't be afraid to pull the chairs in and angle them to achieve a conversation area. It is uncomfortable and uninviting to have to bend your neck to make conversation with others in the room.

Place the pieces and sit down, have a 'mock' conversation and gently 'live' in the space before selecting the right grouping. You will be a force to be reckoned with if you achieve a comfortable seating arrangement!

People will enjoy their time spent in your home and leave not quite knowing why it was such a good experience. It is called being 'comfortable.'

Personally, I am uncomfortable in spaces where there are no tables; no coffee tables, no end tables, nothing! Just sit right down, hold your coffee and tough it out!

I don't understand this mentality; it inspires people to leave the space quickly.

Carefully examine the rest of your pieces of furniture. Make sure they do not overwhelm the space by excessive height or girth. Every piece beyond the primary sitting area is an accessory. Make them count!

Hang your pictures and wall decorations at eye level. This is somewhere between 5' and 5'6".

Find one place in the room to place your largest wall hanging that will allow it to shine for you.

If you look around your friends' homes you are likely to discover that someone measured about a foot or a foot and a half down the wall from the ceiling and hung everything. It is impossible to balance a room with those kinds of heights. Eye Level, always!

If you want to visually tie a space together, like the seating arrangement, find a rug that is two feet wider than the conversation arrangement and center it on the rug underneath.

If you have a sofa that looks perfect against a wall, look for something that balances the size of the sofa with the room.

As unlikely as it may seem, an oversized piece like the one pictured below will attract attention not only to your prized sofa but also to the entire room as it becomes the focal point.

Eliminate clutter, place only large items on the floor as a part of your décor get rid of 'foo foo' pieces that collect dust (a nice curio cabinet is good for these to be displayed).

Your best wall hanging, a flat TV enclosed in cabinetry that can be closed off at will, something that says I'm special!

If you don't see the perfect piece, head to the 'Barely Get Along Street District' in your town! You know what to do!

Add candles in at least one area of your living room. When things are quieter in the house candles are very comforting to relax with.

I think you are ready now to 'strut your stuff' in your living room! Invite your friends and enjoy!

Create a special corner in any area
and let the lighting and mirrors set a
special mood!

Chapter 19
Into the Night

Master suites should look and feel special. By virtue of the name 'Master' someone special sleeps there. You!

Typically a master suite centers on the tastes of two people; many times both are very different. The rule of thumb here is to avoid ruffles and severe masculine lines.

The challenge is to strike a balance between a very sensuous private space, the lion's lair, and a restful, harmonious and peaceful place to allow your body to recover and be ready for the next day.

Hopefully you are able to get your partner to join in the paint and lighting selections. Both are vitally important to arrive at the proper conversion of this space from humdrum to spectacular. If they fail to join in they lose the privilege of complaining!

You gain the home team advantage!

Take a long and critical look at your furniture. Pay attention to the color of the woods and the design. Then start as we did in the living room, with a tape measure and your sketch pad.

Sketch the room including the windows and doorways. Try to arrive at a good perspective of where they are placed in proximity of the entire room. Make notes!

Now, set the practical things aside, close your eyes, and dream. How do you want this special space to feel?

What is important to you? What colors come to mind if you allow yourself to drift past what you have always had to a place you always wanted to go? There now, head to the Chapter 4 Color Your World section and review what each colors inspires.

The Olympic 'South Pacific' and Sherwin Williams 'Smoke Blue' colors make a beautiful backdrop with all white or yellows and teals bedding and linens. Think about the colors and then go online to the paint manufacturer's sites.

You can upload a photo of your actual room (take the picture when full light is available) and then try the colors. This allows you to see your room, with your lighting and your furniture before you jump in to paint. I love these tools!

Look at your overhead lighting. Try to agree on a beautiful chandelier that sets the tone for your new room. Simple or ornate, just select what inspires a fairytale feeling in you and your partner. You do want to escape, don't you?

Overhead lighting makes a huge statement!

Invest $5.00 in a dimmer switch! This allows you to lower the lights, add candles to the tables in the room and drift away together.

Tips to remember:

a) Always place the bed facing the door.

b) Avoid allowing the bed to face the bathroom if possible.

c) Avoid mirrors on dressers or other pieces of furniture that face directly back at the bed. Mirrors capture energy and project it back to the person trying to sleep. You need to escape from unharnessed energy!

d) Add large plants; palms promote a light, airy and romantic feeling.

e) Space permitting, an upholstered bench at the foot of the bed allows for both of you to sit while removing shoes, etc and also holds blankets and bed linens while you are sleeping.

f) Look for lamps for the nightstands that are a little less practical, more whimsical, for the master suite. Dare to dream and inspire dreams together in the only really private area in your family's home.

g) The master suite should be off limits to the rest of the world! It is your private sanctuary.

h) Heavier wood pieces of furniture, even if they are repurposed, instill a feeling of security in bedrooms. This room is more important than any other to feel safe and protected.

i) Choose window treatments that also can black out the light for those special mornings when you actually get to sleep in.

Look for drapes that can pool onto the floor, making a more romantic statement than tailored panels.

j) No clutter is allowed in this lair! What a bummer to have a beautiful escape littered with shoes, clothes and a multitude of discarded items.

It is so worth keeping your master suite in perfect order! It makes a subliminal statement to your subconscious mind. A 'wow, this place is special' kind of statement.

k) Unless you have absolutely no choice, discard those outdated mirrored closet doors.

Head back to the 'Barely Get Along Street' district if necessary, look for paneled closet doors that continue the message of being in a VIP space.

l) If you have a dresser that has mirrors attached above, think about removing them and hanging them on a separate wall.

Then hang something really special above the dresser that is a reflection of you and your partner. Something you both have an affinity to or a favorite photo blown up into a poster and mounted for special hanging.

m) Try to place the TV in a cabinet or something enclosed; these create more energy interference while you're sleeping!

n) Space permitting, find two chairs that are reflection of the two of you and create a small sitting area to relax with a favorite glass of wine or a great book.

Drape the wall behind the chairs, even if there are no windows. Texture and contrast create a cozy, special feeling.

Have an open discussion about the closet and drawer space. Come to a solution that suites both you and your partner, then keep your agreement.

It is offensive when anyone encroaches on your space, making you feel inconsequential.

Those are terrible feelings to take to your master suite and a really bad place to take a special relationship! Be respectful of the feelings of your partner in this special room.

If you have a master bath, select a color that compliments, not matches your bedroom.

Review Chapter 14 'Splish Splash Time for the Bath' and look for ideas that may work in your master bath. I think every master bedroom and bath should feel like a retreat. This means spa time in the bath time and space.

When this room is completed you will have designed a very special space that is peaceful, harmonious and sensuous!

Perfect.

Chapter 20
Knock, Knock, Let Me In...

Time for the guest quarters or just a simple guest room!

Guest spaces are all about comfort. If you're entertaining a friend or family member they either remember the incredible décor, the mattress that allowed them to sleep like a dream or, the week they never slept a wink! Avoid 'Grumble Alley' mistakes in the guest area.

Let's work towards making the best memories from a stay at your home.

The best layout for any bedroom places the bed facing the door. It is the same theory that is in place when entering a restaurant; you always want a seat facing the door. This is an instinctive reaction to the unexpected. It is doubly true when sleeping.

A bed that allows your guest to pile up on pillows and watch TV or read is always a plus. Most guests do not get involved in the family's day to day events and need a get-a-way to allow your family the space to continue everyday activities.

The room pictured below was a typical bedroom enhanced with faux brick on the primary wall. Barn siding was used to create the headboard and then washed with white bone finish to create the lighter effects on the wood.

Chandeliers were hung above both nightstands with a dimmer switch to let the guests set the lighting they are most comfortable with.

Guests don't require nightstands with extra storage, only adequate space to place their traveling clothes and accessories.

The best part of the room pictured is the pillows that invite you to come in and pile them up to get comfortable.

If your budgeting is a concern and you do not have a headboard for your guest space, measure the width of the bed and head to your nearest fabric store.

Look for three or four inch foam which is very inexpensive. Buy enough to cover the width of the bed plus an extra 12" to wrap.

Then check out the remnant table and find a fabric that fits the décor you are working towards in this space. Remnants are very inexpensive and sold by the yard, sometimes by the bolt.

Position the bed and mark off the area on the wall with a pencil. Then use your staple gun and staple the foam to the wall to form a tall and thick headboard.

Once the foam is in place wrap it with the fabric and secure the fabric behind the foam with your staple gun.

You now have an exquisite and inviting headboard that beckons your guests to come and lean into! You can add fabric cover buttons to create the tufted look shown in this picture.

There are online directions to create a headboard by using a piece of plywood, foam, batting to wrap the edges and then fabric to wrap the headboard. There are many variations but the point is; you can create a headboard!

These photos show other people's ideas to create a headboard. Some are foam, hollow doors turned horizontally, oriental screens turned horizontally shutters and even a picket fence! Almost anything can work if you give it a try!

The important thing at this point is locating a good, comfortable mattress. If you are lucky enough to have a furniture liquidator in or near your home they offer very good quality mattresses from hotel liquidations. If not, try Craig's List if a new one is not possible.

Night stands for guest quarters can be purchased at a thrift store. They don't have to match in color or design. Just sand lightly and paint to match your desired décor.

Neutrals like Taupe are the best selections for guest rooms. Regardless of what taste a variety of people have, they all gravitate to warm neutrals.

A small desk that holds a laptop computer and a comfortable small chair is a great addition to a guest space. If you have an extra PC available, hook it up and your guests will brag about the hospitality in your home!

An upholstered chair and table with lighting is another good addition to provide a space to relax without being forced to lie on the bed.

Add wall accessories that create a peaceful feeling; seagulls in ocean scenes, gardens with sunlight, anything that is not busy or harsh will create a restful atmosphere.

All accessories in a guest space can easily be pickup up at thrift and consignment stores if necessary.

If your guests have a private bath I am sure they are pleasantly surprised! Opt for a spa like feeling with neutral colors, baskets full of thick towels and candles that invite relaxation.

A small coffee pot and cups with individual packages of cream and sugar are inviting and provide a private wake up treat for your guest.

Overall, this should be a neutral, natural and relaxing space!

Chapter 21
Kids are People Too!

When you are ready to tackle your children's rooms, I urge you to refrain from seeing them as 'just the kids' for a moment.

Try to mentally step into the person they are becoming to help you can create a space becoming to and fit for a future king or queen!

Children's rooms provide a more restful atmosphere if they are muted shades of your child's favorite colors. If you do not have a separate area for them to play in, avoid bright yellows, reds and oranges if you expect them to actually sleep in there.

Children quickly pick up the subliminal message of energy and those colors promote energy. This makes bedtime a tough sell in high energy atmospheres!

Space providing, aim for a separate bed for each child, a twin is fine or a bunk if necessary. The idea is to provide their own bed for them to claim. It is the beginning of independence.

Your child's room should have a work space for school projects and creative pursuits. Every child needs a room that feels secure, inspires creativity and promotes rest. What a challenge!

Additional storage is a little easier to add in a child's room. You can add small dressers or shelving units to the closet floor enabling them to reach the spaces where they are required to store toys and other personal possessions.

If you fail to address this you will soon discover that their idea of cleaning up their space is to throw everything under the bed where they can no longer see it. Things are relatively simple in a child's world.

Insist on order in your child's room. This promotes learning responsibility which is essential to your child growing into an emotionally healthy adult.

Take them with you to shop for lamps and wall accessories. You will probably have to temper their urges but both of you can arrive at a point of agreement and your child will have participated in his or her own success in arranging their personal space.

These things matter to children who rarely have the final say in decisions at home.

Avoid window treatments that present a 'café' effect. Your child will feel far more secure with thick drapes that close out the darkness and offer a hug at bedtime.

Open the drapes wide in the morning and 'Let the sunshine in!" This is another trick at teaching your child to feel secure in their surroundings.

A small nightlight chases away the scary images a child conjures up in the darkness when they are alone. Let them help you choose one that feels right to them.

Insist on your child maintaining order in dressers and chests and storage spaces in their room. This makes it an easy proposition to let them lay out their favorite choices for school without calling in a search party!

Find a bulletin board that you both agree on for the children's space. This provides a special place to display their work and show it off.

Look for a way to hang mirrors down to your child's level so they are able to see how they look in the choices they have made while dressing for school and other events.

Children routinely fall and get hurt attempting to reach mirrors placed at adult heights. Hanging one on or behind a door is a good way to avoid those falls.

Avoid placing candles or any other accessory in your child's room that promotes fire or any other danger. It is important for them to have their own space; safely.

Chapter 22
All In the Family

If you have a larger home that offers a 'family room' you have already discovered that this is the gathering place for everyone in your family.

These rooms are typically located in the back of the home with easy access to the kitchen and back yard areas.

Your goal is to move the traffic in your home, gracefully, through the space and eventually outside to enjoy fresh air and sunshine.

Most family rooms center on a large TV that allows the family to enjoy special movies or sports together.

Large overstuffed furniture that is comfortable and durable works best in these spaces. Expect family and guest alike to put their feet up, relax and let loose in this space.

Tables in your family room should be equally durable and able to withstand glass rings from drinks and food as many people travel to this room with plate and glass in hand.

Tiled and glass tabletops are perfect for this. Locate some used tables and finish to your desired color and add 2 or 3 coats of poly to seal it or and add your own tiles to create a unique look and feel in this space.

You can also get creative with paint colors in the family room, although, neutrals and earth tones tend to work best here.

Window treatments should be more casual and invite relaxation. Long loose drapes that slide easily open and closed for sliders yet still close out light for special TV programs will be welcome.

Space permitting, a game table is a welcome addition to the family room. This allows people who are not focused on the TV programs to enjoy spreading out with their projects and joining the family while participating in their own activities.

Place furniture in groupings that focus on the activities you expect to be most inviting to your family as they relax and let their hair down.

If you have a combined kitchen and family room space, you can add seating and a place for food that keeps it in the kitchen by adding base cabinets and a tabletop or remnant granite on top to create a bar area. Add seating that you can locate at thrift stores and you have an entirely new look and feel in your space!

Find soft cushions for the sofas that inspire a nap or relaxing with the news or sports.

Larger cushions work best in this space, allowing the younger members of the family to throw them on the floor and cuddle for TV shows.

The family room is all about a comfortable place to do the things you enjoy the most in your spare time.

Plants and trees add to creating a relaxing atmosphere in the room.

Candles should be placed higher so children are not attracted to areas that may be dangerous for them.

Wall accessories should be more casual and can also be more substantial to compliment the larger furniture selections. Then, relax and enjoy!

Chapter 23
Don't Want to Miss a Thing?

America has a long history of 'community' connections. It began in our pioneer days when helping one another with protection and ranching was necessary.

Our earliest homes reflect the inevitable 'front porch'. It is an American heritage!

Depending on your location you probably have a porch, enclosed porch, patio or lanai to enjoy the outdoors.

If you want to reconnect with your neighbors or the community, head to your front porch or whatever outdoor space your home offers.

These spaces can and should become an extension of your home. Family members and visitors can spill out onto these areas to relax and enjoy whatever 'nature' your location has to offer. If you live in a metropolis 'jungle' help is on the way!

A few years ago I went to L.A. on a business venture. My niece lived in Newport Beach, CA so the trip provided some time to 'catch up' and visit with her.

She lived on an upper floor, directly on the beach but facing the street. My impression of Newport Beach is that every street is busy!

At the front of her apartment she had a never used porch that looked out over the traffic and smog.

She was also very unhappy with the layout of her home and was looking for changes that made it more 'user friendly.' Because she was renting she was not interested in spending exorbitant amounts of money to make it feel like home to her.

While she was literally a few short steps to the beach and ocean, she had no way to enjoy the outdoors without leaving her home. She had many friends and enjoyed entertaining at home, not necessarily on the beach.

The challenges for her were the amount of traffic, the lack of any view and for the most part, she found her 'porch' to be utterly distasteful!

We headed to the IKEA store and picked up woven mats in sections of 4' by 6'. These are easy to trim back if you want to cover an entire area since they consist of 1' squares woven together.

Outdoor blinds were available in matching natural colors. We picked up enough to cover her entire open areas without breaking the bank.

Since our choices seemed to leading towards an Oriental look we went over to the lighting area and pick up rice paper shades to add to the overhead light and matching shades for the lamps we intended to use out on the porch.

We headed back to her home with our goodies and in a few short hours her never used porch was transformed into a beautiful and usable space.

We hung the blinds and lifted them high enough to allow the natural light in and low enough to afford a private space for her to enjoy.

A quick walk through in her apartment led to our gathering pieces of furniture that she would not need after our 'redo.' We added these to her porch décor. We took a little used microwave cart from her kitchen, painted it, inserted inexpensive accordion style fold out wine bottle holders and added it as a wine cart.

Candles and more candles were placed on the tables; two large silk trees were added to complete the cozy atmosphere. Suddenly her unused porch (an urban blight was her description) was transformed into one of the most enjoyable spaces in her home.

Beauty is where you create it!

Early morning hours were spent sipping coffee and reading the paper; evening found her popping wine corks with her friends; sharing cheese and bread over candlelight.

We spent about $200.00 to arrive at this transformation. She became very familiar with her community simply by spending time outside on her porch!

Everything is possible if you allow yourself to explore what you do have, what you can affordably acquire and how it can be used to create the space you desire.

The first order of business is to define the space. Where is it, what activities can it be used for and what would you like it to add to your life.

The small front 'stoop' (this is typically a small concrete pad with a tiny roof over it) may feel very limited to you.

However, you must decide what you want the entrance to your home to say to the outside world and how much it can add to your lifestyle.

The stoop is either going to become a part of your entry; or it will be the entry stopping point for the space you create.

If you elect to simply use it to welcome guests, either power wash or paint the stoop and step(s) in a color that works with your exterior color.

If your front door is not the door of your dreams, paint it and shine or replace the hardware.

Add something at the front of your home that makes it distinctly yours. Large pots or yard decorations or plants alongside the stoop extend the eye beyond the small stoop and help you say this is a special place.

Another solution is to head out to your best home improvement spots and pick up paver stones that are very inexpensive. These come in many sizes, shapes and designs; find one that gives a hint as to what is inside the door.

Pick up a couple of packages of black plastic in the paint department of Wal-Mart for under $8.00 while you are out. (Other stores have this plastic but charge twice as much)Add a few bags of sand, mulch or gravel to your list.

Back home you will need to walk off and layout a section of your front yard to create your new space there. Once you feel comfortable about your idea, locate a good rake and remove rocks and large protrusions to create a somewhat level foundation.

Lay the black plastic down across the area you will be using and secure it. (I used long nails several times!) You can trim the paper with a box cutter if you want curves in the design.

You can cut and X into any area where you would like to pant a bush or flowers and dig the hole and plant the addition.

Lay your paver stones out, placing them in a pattern that works for you; then open the bags of sand, mulch or rocks and spread them across the entire area, allowing it to penetrate between the paver stones.

You can add $0.97 outdoor solar lights around the border to create a lighted terrace that leads to the stoop. Add large plants, the seating of your choice and suddenly the front stoop had been transformed into a beautiful entry with outdoor space to enjoy your community. Total costs for this project is under $100.00 if you have available furniture to use outside!

If you have a large porch, clean it and spray or power wash to remove grim that accumulates from wind and weather. You can easily paint it to match your exterior colors if you believe that will help to create your living space.

If not, look at some of the products that can withstand weather, like the inexpensive woven mats. You can separate a small table and chairs from an additional seating area by placing the mats under the table.

Humans are visual creatures.

Space looks and feels completely different to us if the eye is broken by a change in color, texture or patterns. It likewise extends what we perceive as the space in any area by the final break point such as a wall or, outdoor, where the design stops.

Use this to your advantage. Create breaks with this technique or extend space by avoiding them.

Porches are a little more secure than an open area.

You can add overhead lighting to create any atmosphere, hang lanterns for effect or even place very attractive, faux wood tables or other weatherproof accessories that are very attractive out on your space.

In every instance, lighting, flooring and placement of the furniture alter the appearance of your space and transform the look and feel you will derive from it. Treat your covered front porch exactly as though it is a part of your home; changing only the things that require weatherproofing.

An enclosed front porch should be treated as though you have acquired a parlor! Refer to the entry suggestions in Chapter 15 in this book.

Lanai's or enclosed patios are typically much larger than porches. Many span the entire length of the home, and are usually located at the rear of or on the side of the home.

If you are one of the lucky people who have sliding glass doors that can be opened to expose the screens behind them; you have the best of both worlds!

Your space can be treated as an indoor space with respect to fabrics and accessories. Glass enclosed porches or lanais can hold wooden tables for games or an outdoor eating experience, an array of overhead lighting to set any mood and can be draped with any material to create a private space when desired.

Tile is usually a good choice on lanais. It can be cleaned easily and works to extend the feeling of an extension of the home.

Enclosed lanai's can be used for real plants or trees since they provide controlled sunshine levels and protection from the elements. They work equally well with silk trees and plants! The following photos show the lanai of a second floor condo on the lake. The room is not large and the owner elected to use paint on the floor, but still managed to create a restful place to share meals and visits with her friends.

On this lanai curtain rods were hung from the ceiling with wire, grapevines were used to bring the outdoors in and fabric shower curtains moved freely to create privacy or allow sunlight in.

Miniature Christmas lights were strung along the top of the wall, creating a romantic and enchanting space to entertain.

Those tiny lights and candle light combined to provide enough light to take the nighttime picture of this lanai.

Ceiling fans are perfect for lanais and covered porches. Choose one that helps to define the look you want to create.

If you have a screened lanai or patio, you can create a living space that offers weatherproof seating without having to choose the typical outdoor lawn furniture with plastic cushions.

The tables shown below were picked up from a restaurant with a Key West theme. We were able to use these to create a beautiful, casual and user friendly space for entertaining.

Children loved the picnic table while the adults preferred the bar tables. You can take any table that fits your ideal, picked up from a thrift store or yard sale and create this look. Find favorite photos, glue them down and apply 2 or 3 coasts of poly to weatherproof the finished product.

Add a grill and some wood pieces for conversation areas, trees and plants and your friends will walk away talking about your incredible space!

Outdoor lanterns, low level solar lighting at the center of a group of trees and plants and paver stones can be added to the exterior of base of your patio. This extends the eye to enlarge the area.

Privacy fences can be added but they break the space completely, creating a closed room effect.

Look for large boulders to stack and create an interest point. You can also head to your lumber supplier and pick up two pressure treated 1 x 6 inch boards and several pressure treated 1 x 4 inch boards.

Create a base from the six inch board, nail the one inch pieces into angled slats and then attach the other six inch board to the top. You can spray with Min Wax stain and anchor the wall to the edge of the patio.

You have created privacy, a place for the vines to trail and climb and still have an open feeling in your space.

Most people prefer to paint the patio slab as opposed to tiling it. Your patio is exposed to outdoor wind, rain and snow allowing dirt to pile up and stick to the grout.

Outdoor lanterns mounted to the exterior wall of the home help set the mood in these spaces.

Chapter 24
Crowded Spaces, Lonely Places

show off a streamlined space

When families outgrow their space or even singles make one too many shopping trips, you begin to adopt the idea that 'cleaning' means finding one more place to jam things and close the door quickly before it falls out.

If you have long since tired of trying to cram your 'stuff' into a space that simply won't budge; you may appreciate some ideas to try.

Clutter makes people uncomfortable in your home. It makes you uncomfortable there too. I have tackled this many, many times while helping others claim their space. This is a re-claim in my opinion.

Many times people are offended by the thought that their prized possessions are now grouped into a 'clutter' category. The problem stems from having insufficient special places to let these items show off and say 'I'm special'.

Before we move on to create more storage, take a good, hard look around you. If you cannot see any time in the near future that you will want to display or use the offending items, revisit Chapter 17 and the 'Barely Get Along Street District' in your town.

Your unwanted or unused 'stuff' has value! You will not be nearly so upset at letting it go if you are able to recoup the value. If that is of no interest to you, donate it to a worthy cause in your area. A load will literally and figuratively be lifted off your back.

Back to the task at hand; next separate things that are seasonal and then separate clothing and items that can be placed in smaller areas.

Your local discount department store sells very large, moving size, zip lock bags. These are perfect for storing clothing and shoes.

Zip the bag shut and it is airtight; your things are protected. Attach the hose of your vacuum cleaner to the bag with a one or two inch opening and flatten it out.

These babies are flattened out and are going under the bed!

Unused pictures, posters and anything flat can be stored against the wall behind desks, chests, dressers etc. This keeps them safe and out of sight. (Save that under bed space for bigger items.)

Next, select all the items that you cannot, under any conditions part with; and, you don't want to use in your décor.

These get wrapped with brown packing paper or newspaper and boxed tightly. If you treasure them that much, they are worth packing carefully. Use the smallest possible box to safely accomplish this task.

The top shelf of closets and cabinetry over the refrigerator is a good place for these small boxes.

You rarely use the ends of the top shelf of closet space and almost never open the ones above the refrigerator. Duffle bags help hoist these items to the top in lieu of boxes.

If your closet space in unavailable due to a host of shoes, hanging shoe bags are very inexpensive and free up the floor space in your closet.

Look for low dressers and tables at thrift stores, bring them home, paint and move them into the closet to increased storage for things you need occasionally.

If you have an attic space of any kind, the boxes can also be stored there. If you do not have an attic, larger boxes are a little bit more challenging.

For the larger items and larger boxes, look carefully at the ends at the bottom or floor area of your closet space.

Normally this is a more difficult place to reach into. We tend to hang clothing we rarely use at the ends for this very reason. This space is perfect for larger boxes. Stack them if need be.

You should now be down to the things you either want to show off as an accessory or need accessible to use.

Split them up again, into these categories.

If you have plant shelving in your home (vaulted ceilings almost always offer these) you should consider this area as a built in display area.

It is always high in the air so keep that in mind. Small things will disappear up there. Get creative and ask a friend to help you lift the accessories up to the space.

I have used large pots, birds and bird houses, grape vines, baskets, paintings, dolls and a multitude of other things to make this space special. A contrasting color of paint on the plant shelving area helps to attract attention to the area and the things displayed there.

Large silk plants and things that overwhelm your space can fit nicely there. String the miniature lights across the base of the area and you have an entirely new look.

If you do not have this extra space, look around you. Do you have a corner or an area where you can add it? Shelving wrapped around a room is not the answer; you can however, create a special place, in the air in a corner with glass shelving or any kind of wood that matches your décor.

Corners are rarely used except to stick things in that we don't use. Yours can become a spectacular part of your design, layered if necessary.

If you have an area available in your hallway or other corner to add a piece of furniture that can attractively manage display items, take a stroll through your home and then the thrift stores to locate an inexpensive and good quality piece.

Any piece that has potential can be repurposed to fit your décor! Now your 'stuff' is an essential part of your décor!

Putting things in place, eliminating clutter and freeing up space in your home is well worth the time taken.

Once you complete this process you will begin to notice that friends seem more comfortable, stay longer and enjoy their time with you.

More important, you enjoy your time at home.

If you have a garage, you have an attic most likely.

Your storage problems are more about getting things in order, identifying what will be stored and then determining what method works for your storage space.

In short order, clear the clutter! Bring your house to order! Everything is easier when you eliminate unnecessary challenges in your home.

Chapter 25
It's All About the Bling!

artful accents

Accessory, by definition, means 'ornament' or 'partner in crime.' Both can apply to your home decor. It's about the display!

When you are searching for accessory items you will be better served by adopting the marine mantra, 'a few good pieces.' This will go much farther to create an inviting and beautiful space than a host of knickknacks and fake silver and gold trinkets.

It has been very refreshing to see trends for home décor move back to appreciating the good quality, barely used treasures from the past.

Large, simple, good quality mirrors grace the walls rather than overtake them. Use mirrors to reflect light and to emphasize a particular piece of furniture.

Avoid placing a shelf underneath the mirror, it adds to the feeling of clutter.

a brilliant reflection

Unless this is a spectacular set from days of old that you really love, don't do it.

Let the mirror make a simple statement, and add accessories to the table. Accessories should be in balance with the weight of the table and the mirror or picture. A fragile, lightweight candle holder will not do justice to heave antique mirror. Vintage pieces with other vintage items will feel a lot more cohesive.

Accessories are compliments to your room and should not overwhelm the theme.

Choose plants and trees with a completed design in mind. Envision the end result before putting it in place. Use your painters tape to lay out space in your home. Then visually step back and mentally live in the space.

Walk around the room just as you would if the furniture and accessories were there. Get a feel for the flow of the space; then move forward.

Rugs are another accessory that should be well thought out. What are you trying to create? Is the rug slippery when walked across? Is it in a place where children or adults may trip and fall because it is there?

Look at all of these issues and then determine whether it is the right size, shape, fabric and design to enhance your well thought out plans!

Use this same attitude with every accessory! What does it do for the space, for your plan and for the room? Every accessory should have a cause to achieve an effect!

When you are finished, remember that odd numbered groupings (3, 5 or 7) are much more pleasing than even numbered (2, 4 or 6) groupings.

It just is!

Many times we shop and find beautiful pieces, over and over again. Try selecting a few good pieces for the room you are creating and box the rest for a new look later.

More is not always better.

This is true throughout your home. Eliminate dust catching knickknacks or put them into a special cabinet to show them off without cluttering your space.

Regardless of what style you select, all accessories work better with clean, clear and concise lines. Although things may not appear to be casually placed, you know for a certainty how much time and thought was put in the careful draping of a piece of fabric!

Children's playrooms and bedrooms are better served by things they can utilize. A hanging chalkboard or bulletin board is useful to them. Pegs on the wall to hold their jackets and rain coats are useful; they are also decorative.

Quick Tips Guide

Most new homeowners - when presented with a bare room - are overwhelmed with possibilities and insecurities of furniture arrangement.

They may stand in the middle of the room, shake their heads, and wonder where in the world to start.

Although I can't tell each of you where you should put what furniture, I can give you some questions which will help you think about how you will use your space and some general guidelines for arranging furniture.

How you use your space:
Look at the entrances to the room. Do you have doors? Do they open in or out? If they open in, you will need to allow room for those to open fully.

Do you use the room as a pathway to another room? Is the room a destination room? In other words, is the room one that people go TO or go THROUGH? If they go through, you need an easily navigable pathway from one room to another.

How do you want to feel in the room? Do you want it to be cozy and intimate? Do you want an open and spacious feel? Furniture in a cozy room tends to be places in closer groups. An open feel needs more space between pieces.

Are you going to use the room for entertaining? If so, you need flexibility in your furniture choices. Extra seating may be placed out of the way and be moved into use when company comes.

Furniture Placement Guidelines:

Between the sofa and side chairs, designers normally allow 48 to 100 inches. But you should adjust the space according to your family's needs. If you feel more comfortable with the chairs closer, or if you are better able to hear conversations, then move them closer.

If you are using a coffee table in front of the sofa, the normal placement is 14 to 18 inches from the sofa. But again, if you have short arms or long legs, adjust the table until you are comfortable.

For television watching, the normal guideline is to place the television at three times the size of the screen. But with some of these new big screen TVs, three times the size of the screen is in the next room!

Three feet of space is recommended for traffic lanes. But if you have large family members or lots of kids, I would recommend allow an extra foot for safety for your furniture and for your family members.

In the dining room, an average adult needs a depth of 20 inches for a dining room chair, plus 16 inches to scoot the chair back from the table. Again, adjust the measurements to fit your family.

At the dining table, you should allow 24 inches per person or more. If your family tends to gesture as they eat, as mine does, allow another six inches.

In order to serve your guests, allow 46 inches between the wall and the dining table.

For ideal bed placement, allow at least 24 inches between the bed and the wall to get out of bed comfortably and allow 36 inches between the end of the bed and the bedroom or bathroom door.

As you can see, these guidelines are approximate and should be adjusted for your family. Keep in mind, however, that if you are entertaining guests, your placement will require further adjustments for their comfort and ease of movement.

Small Spaces:

If you can stand in the middle of your room and touch the walls on all four sides, you are going to have to use some magic to add visual space to your room. While that magic probably won't involve the overnight makeover of your space by budget decorating elves, here is some slightly less than elfin visual ideas to help your room look larger:

Light Values: Use light values when painting your room. That does not mean you are doomed to white walls! Try light green or cream beige for a feeling of space.

Vertical Space: Use vertical space for storage. Add a hutch or floor-to-ceiling bookcases as a storage solution to reduce the amount of floor space taken.

Up Against the Walls: Place the larger pieces of furniture against the walls, so the open space in the middle isn't broken up.

Open Arms: Choose a sofa and chairs with open arms and exposed legs. This allows light to filter under the furniture, making the room appear airier.

Scale Down: Consider smaller scale furniture. A sofa or bed that takes up less area will help visually open the room.

Reflections: A large mirror in the room will reflect light around the room. This is especially effective with near a window so the outdoors can be reflected.

Angles: Arrange furniture at an angle if possible. This gives visual interest to the small space.

With some imagination and some rearranging of furniture, you can make any room appear much larger than its actual size.

More Room Design Tips

Furnishing a small dining room can present a challenge, as any small space can be challenging. However, you may very well end up having a more efficient and attractive space since a small dining room can force you to focus on exactly what you need.

Consider Scale

Scale might very well be the single most important factor to consider especially when you are furnishing a small dining room. Your dining furniture should be scaled according to the space you have.

Select a Limited Color Palette

A limited color palette may be a good place to start. It is easier to work with a lighter or neutral color palette as it can make your room look airier. Contrasting or complementary colors should only be used as accents.

This is the safe approach. If you are confident around colors, a bold color scheme may work just as well. The trick is not to get too fussy, and just keep it simple.

Use Mirrors

A mirror is a small room's best friend. It opens up space like nothing else. Use strategically placed mirrors on the wall. Using more than one can be an even better idea.

Simple Window Treatments

Simple window treatments help keep fussiness away. Ornate swags and valances could be distracting and too overpowering in a small space. Simple panels could do the job nicely. If you need more privacy, layer with good quality blinds.

Select the Best Table Shape

A round table is the best pick for a small dining room. You might want to pick one with an extension leaf if you have enough space to open it. Otherwise a simple round table will do in a square room.

Pedestal bases are great because you can fit extra guests around the dining table without table legs getting in the way.

A narrow rectangular table might work well in a narrow dining room. The idea is to leave enough space for people to move around easily.

Pick Armless Chairs

Armless chairs work best in a small room

as arm chairs require more room. You might also want to pick chairs that have a more slender profile. The idea is to take up as little physical or visual space as possible.

Consider Transparent Furniture

Transparent material such as glass, Plexiglas, or acrylic can make your dining furniture "disappear" leaving you with lots more visual space. Remember, though, that this is more about appearances than anything else. You will still need to measure to make sure that you leave enough space for people to maneuver easily.

Use a Small Profile Chandelier

A large or fussy chandelier could take up too much visual room. Pick something with simpler lines and a small profile. It would make your space appear larger. Remember it is all about scale.

Arranging furniture is mostly about using empty space around your furniture to create flow in your floor plan. You want people to move around comfortably without bumping into furniture and sit down comfortably without grazing their knees or feeling hemmed in.

Living Room

For your living room to be comfortable, make sure you don't crowd your space. Too much furniture crammed into too little space or sparse furnishings in a room that is too large can make for a very unattractive space.

You need to provide enough space for an efficient flow of traffic, and let your space breathe visually.

This creates a sense of well being and relaxation.

Traffic Lane: 3' or more

Foot room between sofa or chair and edge of coffee table: 1'.6".

Floor space in front of chair or sofa for feet and legs: 1'.6" to 2'.6".

Dining Room

To enjoy your dining room to the fullest, make sure you leave enough space around the table so that people can get in and out of their chairs comfortably and the person who is serving can move around the table without trouble.

Space for occupied chairs from edge of table to back of chair:

1'.6" to 1'.10"

Space to get into chairs: 2'.6" to 3'

Traffic path around table and occupied chairs for serving: 1'.6" to 2'

If you're using armchairs, remember to add two inches to the measurements.

Bedroom

In a bedroom, place furniture so that you don't stub your toes should you need to get up in the middle of the night.

You should also be able to move around comfortably to make the bed and be able to open any drawers without trouble.

Space for making bed: 1'.6"

Space between twin beds: 1'.6" to 2'.6"

Space in front of chest of drawers: 3'

Getting into or out of bed: 2'.6"

Around the House

Leave enough space around the doorways, or the room may look very unwelcoming, and crowded. You always want to leave a small transitioning area uncluttered by any furniture when moving from one area of the home to another.

Space from doorway to first object: 3'

Space around main entrance: 4'

Just because you live in a small space it doesn't mean that you have to use small furniture. You will find that many times, using large pieces when decorating small spaces can actually make a room look larger, rather than smaller.

Using a lot of small pieces of furniture can make it look like you're trying to cram too much in and the room can end up look cluttered and cramped. The key to keep this from happening is to use large furniture, but just use less of it.

For example, in a tiny living room rather than trying to fit in a sofa, chairs, ottoman, coffee table and side tables, try using a sofa, a single table or bench, and perhaps a single side chair. If you have the space you can even include a large armoire for storage.

Get rid of excess small pieces and instead include only what you'll actually use. Then try to open up the space with an oversized mirror on one wall (if you can get it across from a window so much the better).

It sounds crazy but it works. Before trying it out; draw up a floor plan on some graph paper or use an online floor planner to experiment with furniture placement.

Simple fixes for small spaces can help you maximize every single inch of your home. The three things that you most need in a small space are function, comfort and style so before you buy anything make sure to look for pieces that provides these three.

Go Vertical: Consider investing in tall furniture. Floor space is precious, and by going upward instead of outward you give yourself extra room.

Use Walls: By adding shelves or wall mounted cabinets you give yourself room for display or storage without using up extra floor space.

Stylish Storage: Buy occasional and coffee tables that provide storage with drawers and shelves. Beds, room dividers and ottomans are some other pieces of furniture that can provide you with extra storage.

Decorative boxes and storage bins can also store seasonal clothing, sporting goods, office supplies or anything else.

Stackable Chairs: Stackable and folding chairs are an excellent way of keeping a supply of seating that you can pull out as you need.

Retractable Doors: Retractable doors that don't open out let you fit armoires and entertainment centers in small spaces with ease.

Try the Kids' Department: Creative use of youth furniture can serve you well as it is designed to fit into smaller rooms. It can also accommodate most adults just as well. For instance, a child's dresser or desk can fit into small areas. And with today's wide selection of styles you are bound to find a piece that matches your own.

Look for Wheels: Many pieces of furniture have wheels, upholstered ones as well as tables and shelves. The ability to easily move your furniture around to where you need it can serve you well.

Consider Leaves: A full-size dining room table might be too big for your dining area. Look around for one that has removable or retractable leaves.

Even though all of these issues were covered in various places in this book, a handy dandy reference guide makes things move swiftly if you're in a bind!

Chapter 26
Tools of Our Trade

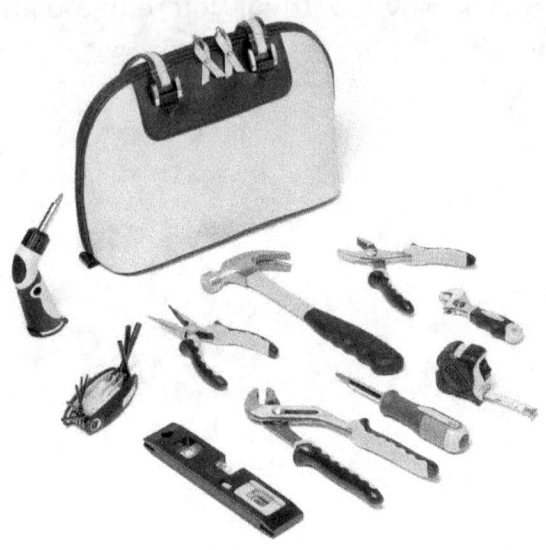

This little pink tool kit is sold on Amazon.com; a host of other options and add on's available. You can also head to Harbor Freight, if your city has one, and find unbelievably good deals on tools.

Or, of course, you can and should shop at the stores and sites that you are familiar with that have great prices!

Regardless, **YOU need a tool kit!**

A good heavy weight hammer, a battery powered screw gun, a nail gun, tape measure, at least two rolls of painters tape, glue gun, coaster to move furniture, paint brushes and rollers and a small and medium size level are essential to any homemaker!

These tools have nothing to do with plumbing, electrical, HVAC or any other BIG job.

These tools are necessary to properly hang a picture, layout a room, or to determine the size of drapes, pictures or anything else you intend to hang or display.

Yours does not have to be pink or matching anything, it does have to be filled with the proper tools and you need to learn how to use them!

If you have no experience at all, find a friend, male or female who can help you learn. If not, ask the sales clerk when you purchase them.

You are unstoppable with your trusty tools and the tips you have learned in this book!

Carry On!

Chapter 27
Know When to Fold 'Em!

    We've spent a lot of time discussing how to make existing things work. Now, for the diehards with a bigger vision and who insist they see a better way; we're with you.

    If you see a wall that simply makes no sense to you and are determined to tear it down by yourself, you better know the history on that wall!

    Load bearing walls support your roof. Every exterior wall and some interior walls are load bearing.

Not that you cannot ever remove one, but, a support beam that meets your building code must take the place of that wall when it is moved. (At the same moment)

This is not a guessing matter. If you are sure you know but have a tiny doubt you need to make a quick trip to your attic and check things out.

Up there it is very clear which walls are supporting the roof. Learn to love them or call a building contractor. If you fail to do this you will still be calling a contractor. It is much less expensive this way.

More than one homeowner looks at the placement of a wall and wonders what the heck was in the mind of this builder! It is more common than you might imagine.

Walls in your entry that separate your living area are almost never a load bearing wall.

However, in older homes where roofing trusses were not used, the kitchen is in the back of the house and the living area in the front; and you guessed it, a load bearing wall separates the two.

This is the wall most people want to move or eliminate to expand space.

Check with your county building department before making changes. An owner builder permit is inexpensive, allows you to hire sub contractors and gives you the benefit of the dreaded building inspector.

If you are dealing with a contractor or sub contractor who hates the inspector or frequently talks about getting around the code; you need to win this battle with your shoes and walk away.

The building inspector is on the scene to protect the occupants of the home or building. Anyone who wants to avoid the inspector is cutting corners and not meeting the safety code. These people are your FRIENDS, even when you don't like what they say. Regardless, you will meet their guidelines or tear it out.

Quick Stepping It!

Recently I went through an open house in a very nice subdivision in south Florida.

The home had a large enclosed pool and had been built with a large lanai surrounding the pool.

Somebody who previously owned the home decided to add some square footage to the house by adding a wall across the lanai. Things were probably going really well as it showed nicely; until you opened the slider doors and found a 12 inch clearance before hitting the water in the pool!

I'm sure the home is going to be on the market for a long time. Even then, an appraiser will come when a new buyer attempts to get a loan and the wall will come tumbling down.

Staying within the guidelines of the building codes is a good idea. One way or another, you're gonna do it!

Every community and state is different; for the most part you are safe making painting and interior changes that do not move walls, electrical, plumbing and most HVAC (heat and air) changes without the benefit of a permit.

You can landscape your lawn so long as you do not add plumbing (sprinklers, fountains or pools) all of which may require a permit.

Check your county building codes (posted online) or call the county building department. They are usually happy to tell you up front rather than be called out to make you remove something.

Guess who knows more about the contractors and sub contractors than anyone in your area? Yep, it's the building inspector. He cannot recommend anyone but the expression on his face is very telling.

Better still, you can go to the board of professional licensing in your state and check the complaints that have been filed against any licensed individual.

You're not helpless or a victim unless you choose to be.

Get bids; at least two unless you are sold on a particular contractor's ideas and have seen their work. If that is the case you should negotiate to a price you both feel is fair.

Be present when the inspector comes. You can learn more than you wanted to know by his visit.

Remember, I have been on both sides of this coin, have remodeled homes, sold homes and built homes; I say this is so you will understand the next statement:

Once you have established a relationship with your contractor or sub contractor that you feel good about; get off their backs!

They are overloaded with ensuring that materials are delivered and people who work for them are on the job. They get paid when it is finished.

Anything you are paying prior to the end of the job is for materials and meeting the payroll on your job. Let them do their job. They desperately want to be paid for their work! I promise.

What to do if things aren't going so smoothly? Stay calm. Schedule a meeting with your contractor and take notes. Write down your questions and the answers you are provided.

Ask them to review your notes to ensure that you have correctly taken the information. Date it, insert the location and time of the meeting, ask them to sign it for you and put it into your file.

You have correctly executed a legal document that can be assumed to be a part of your agreement with the contractor.

If things don't improve and you have reasonably allowed the contractor to perform, call another contractor to look at the job. Unless it is terribly botched, a good contractor will not attack another contractor's work.

He may point out things that could be different. If it is really as bad as you feared, you're going to need a new person on the job anyway.

If you determine this to be the case show the new person the notes taken at your meeting.

I want to again caution you not to jump the gun and assume your contractor is worthless and ignorant because you don't like the pace of the job.

They want to finish more than you want them to finish. If things are not moving along, try to rationally determine the reason for delays.

If something is beyond the control of your contractor due to back orders etc. it is also beyond your control.

Just relax!

Early in this book I mentioned the method that my brother, the building contractor used in his business. You may recall that I told you he 'walked through a day in the life' of the home buyers.

Think About It!

One day I brought a couple to see him who had a specific request regarding the dining room. They had purchased a table that seats 12 people and were determined to make the house fit that table!

As I said many times, anything is possible. As we sat around the table my brother looked for the best response to their concerns.

At last he said "Let's add a bay area to the dining room." This would add 5 feet of usable space if the table extended to the bay window. The bay area would cost an additional $4500.00. I thought that was a lot of added expense to accommodate a table.

The owner was insistent that she did not want a mere extension; her dining room was important!

At the end of this meeting, after a great deal of discussion, the owner decided to extend the entire front of their two storied home to accommodate the table. The cost was a walloping $30,000.00!

I personally thought this was foolish, it still bothers me today. I hope the table is a sturdy one that they will use for years to come at that price for the accommodation.

Use your head, not your heart when you are dealing with extensions or changes to your home.

If you get caught up in the dream phase

you will hit the ground with a resounding thump when reality meets you there!

Contractors can make anything happen that you can dream of. Don't tread so far out into the water that you will need a tug boat to get back to dry ground!

Be reasonable, consider costs and the value added and then proceed.

Chapter 28
If It Takes a Village...

Lately we have begun to hear more and more about how creating change takes a community or a village; as though we did not know this!

Americans have a DNA unlike any other nation on the planet! We are a 'can do' nation of people who cannot and do not accept defeat. No has never meant no in American history! No means, 'not that way.' In short, Americans find a way, where there is no way.

We don't worry about odds either. When General Washington led his pitiful, cold and proud troops to defeat the most powerful military presence on earth, he did it with a hope and a prayer. We have been doing it ever since.

Americans are the first and biggest responders to every tragedy around the globe. If an American air carrier breaks the horizon, something big is going to happen.

The USA arrives with aid that feeds nations, manpower that literally moves mountains and a determination to finish the job. And we always do.

This country does not fight wars for the mere acquisition of land; we fight for freedom from atrocities for other people. We arrive to right a wrong. It is a nation like none other!

If you are reading this and you are not American, these traits are what make this country great. They are the best of America and the traits worth pursuing, no matter where you are or are from.

Why then have we lost our good neighbor policy at home?

By the time most of us left the high school graduation, we had begun to notice a little thing in our lives that kept popping up; that what we gave, we received.

It is the boomerang of life. If you want a good friend you must be a good friend. If you want to be loved, you must be willing to give love.

Your home will feel much safer and you will be happier there if you have good neighbors. You get them by being one.

Today's communities rely on 'neighborhood watch committees' to replace what used to be a given; that the people who lived in a community cared about the community and their neighbors.

It is not necessary to become intimately involved in your neighbor's lives. I really recommend you don't!

However, take stock of what your neighborhood consists of. Are young children or pets a part of your street or community? If so, this means controlling speed is essential.

Do you notice a home that has only one parent or a single person living alone?

You are not expected to take the place of anyone missing from someone else's home. If you are willing and able to extend small favors like lifting obvious heavy items or other small things that make a difference, you become a great neighbor.

Most particularly take note of anyone on your street or in your community who is elderly or handicapped.

I have learned that this group of people are very independent and hate appearing to need any kind of help. They are desperately trying to hang onto their self reliant life style. They also need the most.

Things you take for granted like taking trash to the curb become a difficult task with a walker or wheelchair.

Trimming hedges is nearly impossible with arthritic hands and fingers. They simply don't work like they used to. When this begins, opening a vital bottle of medication is a nearly impossible task. Offer to help.

Small things can make a big difference in the lives of your neighbors. If you think there is no good reason for you to worry about it, imagine this as a boomerang that comes back to you when someone like you offers assistance to your parents or grandparents. Life is like that.

If you are planning a party or get together that you know is likely to be noisy or intrusive, talk to your neighbors ahead of the event. Let them know and listen if they have an issue with it, and try to arrive at a solution that makes everyone comfortable.

This is also true for extra parking. Work it out ahead with your neighbors so that it is not an issue in the midst of your event. These are simple courtesies that smooth your path.

If you have a barking animal that rouses the neighborhood during sleep time, make a good effort to gain control of it or bring it inside where it does not disturb your neighbors.

If you live in a subdivision, rather than on a lot of acreage, don't assume that your neighbors will find your monkeys' antics amusing; or that bears, tigers, lions, pythons and boa constrictors or other exotic animals are cute. You need to be on a lot of acreage and acquire an exotic animal permit. You have become a zoo keeper!

Many times the smallest favor is the biggest thing that has happened in another person's life today.

Maybe it does indeed take a village, but this begins in our own back yard, literally, and everyone needs to participate in the success of their village!

Chapter 29
Go Where the Music Takes You

Throughout this book, an obvious (I hope) effort has been made to jog a song or a line from a song from your memory bank. That was intentional.

Music is 'soul food,' it inspires us to let go and to feel. Music has no boundaries; it creates an atmosphere or sets a mood. Music is like an emotional playground. It is also particular to every individual. We all know what makes us feel good and we turn to music under all kinds of conditions.

Most people know exactly what song was popular when any major event happened in their life.

But, did you know... music opens the channels of creativity in your brain? The purpose of this book is to help each person find their own niche in creating a space that is perfect for them; not perfect for a designer, just perfect in their lives!

Everyone is creative; many people just don't tap into that part of their mind. It is a closed door that music slowly opens! So, keep playing the music while you work!

I have to imagine this is where the 'whistle while you work' idea sprang from.

My mother had 6 children. She also maintained a perfectly clean house. Every Monday morning she faithfully removed the old wax from all the hardwood floors and applied new wax.

There were mountains of laundry involved in a household that size. Dryers were not prevalent back then. My mother carried laundry out at 6:00 AM, even on the dark winter mornings, and cheerfully hung the clothes out to freeze dry.

I love homes. I love almost everything about them. I could not, however, understand why in the world anyone would work as hard as she did and never complain.

She made our clothes, taught Sunday school classes, directed the choir and finally went to work at a large newspaper and quietly and without telling us so, was awarded the Governor's Award for Excellence in Journalism.

One day I finally asked her, "Why don't you EVER complain?" It was not natural! I helped as much as I could, we all did, there was just too much to do and still, she did it.

Her response was so simple, "Instead of being resentful, I work for God and for my family that I love."

She said she had never thought much about the volume of work, only that she was thankful to have a home that she could make her family comfortable in.

Maybe most of us feel that way about our parents or someone influential in our lives. They seem to maintain standards that are always a beacon of light in the dark.

My mother played music all the while she was sewing, cooking, canning and getting the next class ready or disciplining all of us children.

I swear it made her smile, and she was anything if not creative in her methods of making us look for a better way to handle the jobs she insisted we do.

We have all heard the axiom that the longest journey begins with the first step; I believe it is begins before that.

I believe that when something matters to us a lot, we harbor a dream, so dare to dream. The dream fans a tiny flame, a pilot light that ignites hope. Hope springs to life when we begin to believe that there might be a way to accomplish the dream.

Once we believe in the dream, we begin to realize that dream.

It is then that the first step in a long journey begins. I appreciate your joining me on this realizing this dream. I hope your 'Make It Mine' experience has provided helpful ideas and information for you to live by and with.

Having a home is an American heritage; having a home you love is an American dream!

We're a nation of dreamers, movers and shakers! Dare to Dream!

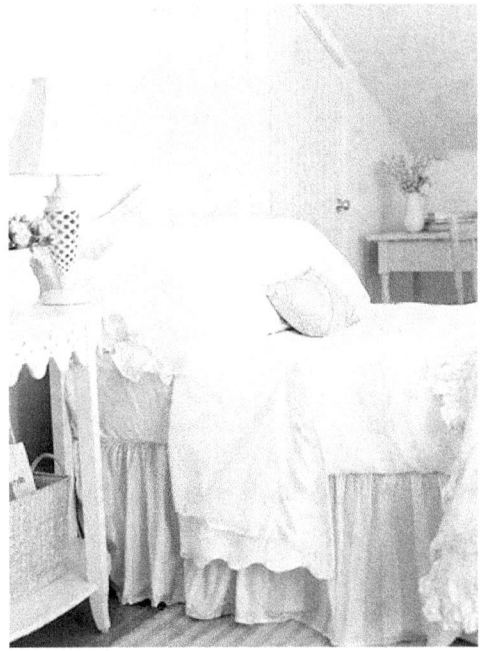

Chapter 30
Companions along the Way

As much as I thought I had learned in this game of life, I seem to be constantly discovering what I did not know. Maybe that happens to you as well!

I lost my father when I was only 13. Perhaps that was the time when I began to 'fast track' my life.

I married young and from that point forward everything moved fast; three sons and a rapid fire succession of changes!

I noticed that my life seemed to be lived on a pendulum that swung wide. If I was blessed with a success it was much more than anyone expected, far exceeding my dreams.

A failure was a dismal one, likely as not to end up on the news. I lived in a small town in Ohio for a large part of my life.

It was my televised Farmingdale Subdivision council meeting that featured the nice country gentleman who stood up in a crowed gymnasium and asked the Mayor how he planned to keep the blacks separated from the whites!

I was sitting beside one of my VP's, who was also black. We were the only two in the room laughing. You simply cannot take some ideas out of some people; nor can you change other people. I learned to accept them and grew to understand them in some fashion.

A car accident that seemed not to be serious took the life of my unborn child.

An accidental bang into the dining room wall exposed a tumor in my hip that resulted in bone marrow grafts and a long, hard recovery.

Everything was extreme!

By the age of 35 I owned and operated a Real Estate Company, Title Insurance Agency, Mortgage Company, Leasing Company and Development Company. All five of these companies were very successful and very time consuming, with 88 employees.

Throughout this time I had three sons who were far more important to me than any of the businesses.

Somehow we made it, although not necessarily as we planned.

Life just seemed to move fast.

I married my childhood sweetheart, and more than 33 years later I found myself in the midst of 25 gallons of gasoline and a box of matches, a SWAT team and a hostage negotiator.

That was a long day. As my husband disappeared in the cruiser and the firemen began foaming my house I knew a change was going to come.

See what I mean? Things are just extreme!

All along the way, some things were constant. My mother was an ever present influence in my life, in the lives of all six of her children.

Among the many very humble things she instilled in her children, she tempered it with the platitude that 'you make dust or eat dust.' Things got fiercely competitive at times! She quietly passed away a few months ago and took our broken hearts with her, for now.

My brother was the lone male child in our family. Somehow he held a different position than the 'girls'. In some manner I always placed him on a pedestal. I found him brilliant and I loved working with him. He was a gentle and fearsome giant!

One night in August of 2009 at the age of 59, he went to sleep and left us forever. The bottom dropped out of my world.

I have laughed and cried and prayed with family, friends, neighbors and clients for years. It is a part of life.

It seems like I have accumulated a 'war chest' of stories about life in general, beginning back with my days as a Rainbow Sweeper salesman to the present.

When extreme is the norm, you will always have great stories! Somewhere about my mid 30's people began telling me to write a book. I laughed it off and always replied, "Someday, when I have the time." (I thought I was very busy you see.)

My family has all played a big part in my life; we are close, maybe clannish. We are loud and gentle and argumentative and consoling and cheer each other on in some manner. I assume every family is like this.

I am the youngest of my mother's six children; I felt pretty invincible. It was I who carried her about the last few days of her life.

I always expected to be the strongest or to find a way to handle any job. I was, after all, the youngest!

One Saturday a few months ago, while I was visiting an older sister's home I woke up and complained of a persistent ache in my back.

It simply would not go away and seemed to have been there for many days. I notoriously avoid doctors at all costs; she knew this. I firmly believe in self healing.

My sister took a long look at me and said, "You're really sick, I mean really sick. We're going to the emergency room."

Much as I hated it, I meekly accompanied her to the ER. No one there appeared very interested and they were really busy.

An X-ray and a CT scan were completed and there we waited. Suddenly a surgeon who was assisting the ER doctor for a moment strode into the room and quickly stated, "Both of your lungs are pretty well shot; the right more than the left. The right lung has collapsed. That is very painful; here's a prescription for Vicadent, it's very painful. You need to see a Pulmonary Specialist."

He barely broke stride, delivered this message and left the room. My sister and

I looked at each other in utter amazement.

The doctor dropped this bomb as though we had been forewarned and expected it.

We went home. Now what? No one seemed to really know what to do with a collapsed lung. What did it mean?

My sister's partner was a former Respiratory Therapist. He had some ideas to offer.

Another older sister was an RN with 12 years of education in the medical field and far more in experience. She had also studied as a Shaman and was uncanny at detecting medical ailments and cures. She had some thoughts to share.

Yet another sister who has a medical background listened and thought it would pass; that maybe it was not so serious. I wanted to believe that one.

My oldest sister was strangely silent.

My sister, who had gone to the ER with me, and I set out to see the Pulmonary Specialist, knowing he would say the hospital was wrong, wrong, wrong! At first he did!

He spent a few minutes looking at my records, talked with me and said this was impossible! Anyone could look at me and see this was a bad diagnosis. He told me the hospital does pretty well but he was the specialists and he was right. He thought it was all a little ridiculous.

Still, I had to return in a week to see what treatment he might need to provide.

I left, relieved and thankful that the hospital was so wrong. I knew it!

But then, there is that history of extremes on the pendulum that has permeated my life.

It is worth noting that I have seen friends and people I genuinely love go, and wondered where the road turned and how I missed the turn; I've lived through enough oddities to think that not much could surprise me.

The following week my sister and I returned to the pulmonary doctor; ready to grab the treatment plan and go to lunch. We thought we were very busy, you know.

The first test was a blood gas test; I saw red boxes and alerts on the computer screen. I questioned the nurse, who laughed it off and said the machine was wrong and obviously not working.

On I went to the hyperbaric chamber testing and everything else in the repertoire of a pulmonary specialist's bag of tricks and tests.

Finally I was finished. The nurse who had performed the first test came to the counter and asked them keep me there while she talked to the doctor.

With a really sinking feeling I went to wait with my sister. I knew something big was coming. I told her so.

She could not imagine what it was. I could never have dreamed it!

Finally I was led to my doctor's office. That was clue number two that things are amiss. It was his office, not a treatment room.

The pulmonary specialist walked in and told me the delay was my fault. He showed me a Band-Aid on his wrist and said he had taken the very painful blood gas test to check his equipment. And lo, it was right!

My life changed on a dime. My oxygen level barely cleared 50. He told me a truck would be delivering oxygen to my sister's home in an hour.

As low as my oxygen was, everyone's oxygen levels drop further while sleeping. It was not safe for me to be alone when sleeping.

I was stunned; my sister was perhaps more so. Somehow we made it home.

Since that time, life has changed to include discussions about research hospitals and test programs and sometimes about transplants.

A week prior to the hospital visit the same sister and I moved all the furniture in her home, including a piano and cleaned and touched up paint, a normal kind of activity in my life.

This was a big deal.

Many, many tests have come and gone and still the doctors are trying to determine the cause; I am trying to live with the effects.

My own castle has temporarily shrunk to the size of my sister and her partner's spare bedroom, which, of course, we redecorated!

But, every adversity has an opportunity. I realized that, at least for now, that elusive commodity called time had arrived in spades! I could write!

My sister's partner played a baby grand piano on many nights. One particular song, 'Three Coins in a Fountain' continued to grab my attention.

I've never heard the original artist version, but his version took the presentation of the last line in the chorus to a place that was powerful, uplifting and filled with hope.

The song is about coins that have been tossed into a fountain with each person hoping their wish would be granted.

The last line in the chorus of that song is
'Make it Mine!'

Could there be a better title for this opportunity to share the things I've experienced, and hopefully to help lift and move the dreams for your dream home into place?

Hardly; I'm in it to win it, this seems to be the biggest mountain to climb so far in this journey!

Perhaps the most important thing I have learned is that life is meant to be lived looking through the windshield and not the rear view mirror. I suspect that is why one is so much larger than the other to provide the best view!

About the Author

Alexa Keating earned a well respected reputation in commercial and residential decorating with a career that began in 1976 and continues through today.

Her home creations helped to create winning residential development projects from Ohio to Florida, most notably remembered by her ability to work with each home buyer to create a home that reflected their unique personality showcased in an elegant and natural design.

Alexa's commercial designs included award winning and much celebrated retail store window and floor displays that were photographed and filmed by an international audience while frequently drawing gasps of surprise and awe, always bringing unsurpassed sales.

Her notable skill in conceptual decors has earned her a reputation as a premiere decorator. Her work was noted in Who's Who in American Women/ Business and Industry over several years.

Alexa's passion for home decor is reflected in the beautiful surroundings that she creates.

Her ability to collaborate with architects, her own group of contractors, and her clients have earned Alexa a well deserved reputation as a true professional.

Born and raised near Cincinnati Ohio and re-locating to Florida in 1999 she continued her pursuit of decor and real estate development in Fort Myers and throughout south Florida, now residing in Fort Myers Florida.

Alexa Keating

Let Go and Let God

As children bring their broken toys
with tears for us to mend,
I brought my broken dreams to God,
because He was my friend.
But then, instead of leaving Him,
in peace, to work alone;
I hung around and tried to help,
with ways that were my own.
At last, I snatched them back and cried,
"How can you be so slow?"
"My child," He said,
"What could I do? You never did let go."

~ Author: Lauretta P. Burns –

Make It Happen!